Table of Contents

15 HOT TOPICS FOR TODAY'S CHRISTIAN

COMPILED BY HAYES PRESS

Published by:

HAYES PRESS

The Barn, Flaxlands

Royal Wootton Bassett

Swindon, SN4 8DY

United Kingdom

www.hayespress.org

CHAPTER ONE: CAN I LOSE MY SALVATION? (GEOFF HYDON)

Does God hold the threat of eternal punishment over born-again believers? Could they lose salvation? These are questions that have long concerned Bible readers and there are many, many Christians today who live in fear of losing their salvation; perhaps an alcoholic drink or saying a swear word would result in God punishing them for ever. Some think God would only do this if the sin was of a very serious type, but He still could. To live in such fear is a desperate plight, and a real one! The Bible leaves no doubt that people who refuse God's offer of salvation through His Son's sacrifice for them do indeed face eternal punishment (1). But that is for unbelievers. Must Christians live in the same fear? Several Bible verses might be understood to say eternal life can be lost. We will examine the most difficult ones in a moment. First let us give great emphasis to the Bible truth that salvation is secure, and cannot be lost. It is something we can be fully confident about, here and now (2).

Here are three very good reasons to have such confidence:

> 1. If our behaviour as Christian believers determines whether we shall remain saved or be lost, that would mean Christ's death would be somehow insufficient to pay for all our sins. Our salvation, cleansing and eternal security would therefore then instead be dependent on our own supplementary efforts, which is the opposite of New Testament teaching (3).

2. The Lord Jesus Christ said that His sheep (the ones He died for) have eternal life and they will never perish (4). Life that is terminated is not 'eternal' life. 'Never' perish can only mean they are always secure.

3. Paul explained that every believer is baptized into the church which is called the body of Christ (5). Ephesians 5:23-27 shows clearly that Christ is able to cleanse and preserve the Body, so those forming that Body are secure. Who could possibly un-baptize a member of the Body and extract them from their life in Christ?

One of the reasons given by those who think salvation can be lost is that Christians would disregard holy living if there were no consequences for sinning. This is a real risk, but it is very poor reasoning. First of all, there are indeed consequences if a believer sins, even though they will not be exposed to eternal punishment. Consider, for instance, Ananias and Sapphira, who selfishly lied to God the Holy Spirit (6). Again, the Church of God in Corinth turned Christ's command to remember Him into a party scene (7). The result was that God sovereignly intervened to cause sickness and death among them. Also, Christians who committed immorality were cut off from their fellow-Christians; the proper objective of Christianity is the perfection of holiness (8) not permissiveness. John makes it very clear that all Christians will indeed sin,9 no matter how we try to avoid it – and try we should! The question before us is not whether we will sin, but do the consequences include loss of eternal life?

It would be poor reasoning to ignore the three points listed above, but it is very good reasoning to still avoid sin at all costs. There are three important factors in this respect:

a. If as a believer I sin, I may well be exposed to suffering, justifiably, as above

b. More than that, I may cause harm or offence to others, so the consequences spread further

c. By far the biggest consequence is the offence to God caused by my action.

Each of these points bears further examination. God may intervene in our earthly lives and even correctly and inscrutably conclude that there is only, on balance, loss to ourselves if He lets us live out a longer permissive life here; so He may take our physical life away. He gave it; He has the right to take it away, as Job once noted. But God evidently desires our lives here to have a positive result that He can reward (10). However, by our actions we can lose the opportunity of eternal reward. Paul, having noted that worthless activities will vanish in the flames of God's assessment, writes...but he himself will be saved ... Perhaps such an outcome is captured in John's warning about being ashamed before the Lord at His coming (11).

Christ, who promised eternal security, certainly did not promote permissiveness. He gave clear teaching on what must happen if I sin against my fellow Christian (12). And what if a Christian sins and non-Christians notice? Will they not develop a low opinion of Christianity and of Christ because of this? Partly for that reason, a church of God may have no option but to cut off a disciple, especially where the sinner has refused to mend his/her ways and truly repent. This is an awful consequence. But what is the divine objective when sin has occurred? Forgiveness and cleansing; and that is what most of Matthew 18 is about.

In reality, only God can secure cleansing from sin; our attempts to stay saved by being blameless would likely fail. So when a sin occurs, God provides a process designed to result in forgiveness in response to repentance, a divine initiative worked out on earth. How sad if God has forgiven the repentant one, but Christian disciples refuse to do so, unable to see a distinction between condoning sin and God cleansing the sinner. But when we sin, we devalue God's salvation. How dare we offend God our Saviour so! Perhaps this is leads into the difficult passages on our subject, which necessitate viewing things from God's perspective. Hebrews 6:6 is often quoted as evidence that Christians can become lost again. But that is not what it says. Verses 7 and 8 can be understood with less difficulty in the context of 1 Corinthians 3:15. God is looking for spiritual prosperity in saved lives; ground that He can bless. But if our waywardness removes that possibility, then the field of opportunity will be cleansed by fire; no works for God are left for Him to reward. How sad! In this context, we can better see God's view of this sinning person: one who regards the shame of the Cross as of no consequence.

Though their fellow-Christians may follow the directions of Matthew 18, there is no repentant response. Repentance needs to be God-given.13 While God is committed to eternally save all true believers, He is not committed to grant repentance to those who go on sinning with a high hand (see Num.15:30-31). Perhaps we should note that the extreme case presented in Hebrews 6 describes Jewish Christians turning back to Judaism, taking their side with those who crucified the King. Another potentially difficult passage is 1 John 5:16-17. Some link this to the unforgivable sin of Matthew 12:32. The answer, in context, is that because the Spirit of God is responsible for new birth, then if Christ's unbelieving hearers were blaspheming by attributing the Spirit's power in His miracles to the Devil it is never possible to simultaneously receive the miracle of forgiveness through Christ. No one can truly accept Jesus as Lord except by the Spirit. Believers may offend the Spirit (and be forgiven) but to become a believer they they must first submit to the Spirit's conviction of who Christ is. But what then is in view in John's statement about a "sin unto death"? How can that be explained?

The text does not address the possibility of forgiveness, but simply focuses on God giving spiritual life to a "brother" who already has eternal life. Believers who have been well-taught about their salvation will know that it can be viewed in three ways:

(1) Salvation from the penalty of sin (which brings eternal life);

(2) Salvation from the power of sin (which enables a Spirit-filled life); and

(3) Salvation from the presence of sin (which occurs when the Lord returns to give immortal bodies to the saints, forevermore free from surrounding sin).

Of these three, does not salvation from the power of sin fit quite understandably in 1 John 5:16? Understanding and applying 1 John 5:16-17 requires spiritual perception, to see things from a divine perspective and order our requests in line with God's will (15). If we apply ourselves to achieving that practical objective, we will focus on the need for a spiritual life of service, not an unforgivable sin. Other scriptures could be considered in a similar way. In each case we should ask if a statement about eternal punishment of believers is being made, or if the scripture is implicitly speaking about loss of an opportunity to serve God through succumbing to the power of sin (16). The context certainly needs to be considered; some scriptures apply to people who do not get saved before Jesus returns and miss out on the current gospel message of God's grace (17); in some places the explanation lies not in the promise of eternal security, but the basis for failing to receive it (18).

And we should always be careful to acknowledge that not everyone who says they are saved actually is saved. If a false profession of salvation is made, the person remains as unsaved as ever; their refusal to obey the gospel (19) means they do not have eternal life, so they remain exposed to eternal punishment.

For a fuller treatment of this subject, please read: 'Once Saved, Always Saved' by Brian Johnston (available from Hayes Press and as an e-book from Amazon)

References: (1) 2 Thess.1:7-9 (2) 1 Jn.5:13 (3) Eph.2:8-9; Rom.3:20-23; Jn.6:39-40; 1 Jn.1:9-2:2 (4) Jn.10:11,28-29 (5) 1 Cor.12:13; Jn.1:33 (6) Acts 5:1-10 (7) 1 Cor.11:20-34 (8) 1 Cor.5:9-13; 2 Cor.7:1 (9) 1 Jn.1:8 (10) 1 Cor.3:13-15 (11) 1

Jn.2:28 (12) Matt.18:15-35; 1 Jn.1:6-9 (13) 2 Tim.2:25 (14) 1 Cor.12:3 (15) See Vine's Complete Expository Dictionary on 'Ask' Gk. erotao. John's use in 1 John 5:16 implies we cannot approach God with a proposal that He might be wrong, and ask Him, as though we were His equals, to change His mind! (16) e.g. Gal.6:8,9 and see Rom.6:22 and comparable passages (17) e.g. Matt.25:46 (18) e.g. Rom.2:7-8 (19) Heb.5:9

Bible quotations from the NKJV.

CHAPTER TWO: DO I NEED TO BE BAPTISED TO BE SAVED? (BRIAN JOHNSTON)

As I write this, I'm in a country where 'baptismal regeneration' is a widely held doctrine. For any who have not encountered this, it's the belief that water baptism (as distinct from baptism in the Holy Spirit (1)) is necessary for someone to become a child of God, to have new life, and to obtain salvation from the penalty of their sins. In what follows we will defend the Bible's teaching – from Romans chapter 6, for example – that believers' water baptism is a public recognition of an inner change previously brought about by God through faith on our part. Upon baptism, the Christian believer resolves to live to please the Lord. I well remember my first attempt at outlining orthodox New Testament teaching on Philippine soil. It was June 2003 and the room was comfortably full with some 40-50 persons giving rapt attention, and with their Bibles open. I was speaking through an interpreter and this, although accurately done, elongated the process.

The feature, however, that really lengthened the study was its thoroughly interactive nature. I was still covering 'first base' on the New Birth when the first interruption came. "Born of water and the Spirit (2): doesn't this reference to water allude to a believer's baptism in water? And does it not prove that such a baptism is a required part of what it means to be re-born? And in this way we possess salvation from the penalty of our sins?" It should not seem strange to us that this opinion is encountered.

It has a long history, stretching back, it would seem, at least as far as 110-165 AD and the time of Justin Martyr who wrote: 'He that, out of contempt, will not be baptized, shall be condemned as an unbeliever ... For the Lord says: "Except a man be baptized of water and of the Spirit, he shall by no means enter into the kingdom of heaven"' (3).

Speaking elsewhere of those under instruction, he said: 'Then we bring them to a place where there is water, and they are regenerated in the same manner in which we ourselves were regenerated' (4). The problem with this interpretation of John 3:5 is that it makes an inaccurate assumption that 'born of water' refers to water baptism. Is there a better way of understanding the Lord's combined use of water and the Spirit in relation to the spiritual renewing of our nature which is a necessary condition for qualification for the kingdom of God?

There is, for in verse 10 of the same chapter the Lord challenges Nicodemus' ignorance of the relevant Old Testament background which Nicodemus as the teacher of Israel was expected (by the Lord) to have understood. Note the reference to 'water' and 'spirit' in the context of inner spiritual transformation that's found in Ezekiel's writing: "I will sprinkle clean water on you, and you will be clean ... and put a new spirit within you; and I will remove the heart of stone from your flesh and give you a heart of flesh" (5). This linking of 'water/washing' to the Spirit's work at (Israel's future) conversion indicates Titus 3:5 is a more helpful clarification of John 3:5. After that first encounter in Davao City, I've repeatedly come across those of different denominations who advocate that, without water baptism, we cannot be assured of divine forgiveness and a place in heaven. Some others, with a kindred spirit to ourselves in seeking to return carefully to the New Testament Scriptures, stumble at the early hurdle of Acts 2:38.

Surely, they say, this verse which talks of "being baptized ... for the forgiveness of ... sins" in order to receive the gift of the Holy Spirit is all the proof we need that baptismal regeneration is an essential part of the established New Testament pattern of teaching? However, before we could conclude that, we must apply the safeguard of comparing scripture with scripture, allowing verses where the meaning is plain, to govern our understanding of texts where the meaning is less clear. Such a survey shows that it's most likely that the verse we've mentioned was some kind of special requirement to attest to the genuineness of faith commitment of those Jews belonging to the generation who had put Christ to the cross. When we compare Acts 10:43 with 19:2, the settled pattern of Apostolic teaching is clarified: forgiveness of sins and receiving the gift of the Holy Spirit are granted to those who believe, prior to their water baptism (which is found in Acts 10:48 and 19:5 respectively).

Paul sends a clear signal in 1 Corinthians 1:17 by saying: "Christ did not send me to baptize, but to preach the gospel." If it is taught that baptism is necessary for salvation, how could Paul make such an emphatic distinction? Generally, advocates of the belief that baptism in water is necessary for salvation rest their case strongly on Mark 16:16. If only subjected to a superficial review, this verse seems to make their case clearly: "He who has believed and has been baptized shall be saved; but he who has disbelieved shall be condemned." If anyone wishes to be contentious on the basis of this verse, they must be faced up with the second part of it which focuses on the critical element of belief alone among those who are not to be condemned. I often point out that I, too, am a baptized believer and I know that I am saved, but the Scriptures (including this one) teach that it's crucially my faith in Christ's atoning death that has saved me from future condemnation before a holy God.

It's also worthwhile pointing out that the concluding section of Mark's Gospel – of which this verse is part – is not found in early New Testament manuscripts. As a result, we can by no means be certain that this is part of the inspired original text. It's foolhardy to base a doctrine upon a singular text whose authority can, at least, be debated. Usually, as the debate unfolds, there comes an anticipated appeal to 1 Peter 3:21 which says:

> "Corresponding to [those brought safely through the waters of Noah's flood], baptism now saves you - not the removal of dirt from the flesh, but an appeal to God for a good conscience – through the resurrection of Jesus Christ."

It's necessary to think rather carefully here. At the time of the devastating, worldwide Flood in the days of Noah, the ark was the vehicle to save its occupants from the watery judgment; but the waters themselves were the vehicle that saved the very same persons from the previous corrupt world. The former seems to typify salvation from the penalty of sins; and the latter, salvation from a corrupting society in which we may in all good conscience have to endure suffering when doing what is right. Only in this last sense does – or can – baptism be said (correctly) to 'save' us. A baptized follower of the Lord Jesus can helpfully consult their conscience regarding their intended actions: is this activity consistent with my advertised identity as a follower of Christ? And with this, Acts 22:16 can be satisfactorily shown to be in agreement.

Let's look at the verse: "... be baptized, and wash away your sins, calling on His name." Set at the time of Saul's dramatic conversion, these are the words of God's servant, Ananias. Saul had encountered the risen Christ on the Damascus highway. He too, had been a high-profile opponent of the Christian persuasion, and it might be argued (as in Acts 2:38), that the public act of water baptism was accordingly and again exceptionally required of him. It's not necessary to understand the text in that specialized way, however, but in a way that applies to all believers. Believer's baptism is intended to be a watershed event in one's life (6).

By saving faith we are not the same person we once were in God's sight (7) and following our water baptism we are not to live as we once lived (in our sinful past lifestyle) (8). So, the washing of Acts 22:16 can be viewed as the cleansing of our ways, the removal of past vices, and the demonstration of a new lifestyle no longer dominated by obvious sin. In a land like the Philippines where the teaching of Ephesians 2:8-9 is so effective against the error of a reliance on good works for salvation, it's sometimes found to be helpful to observe that baptism as a rite or ordinance, is a 'good work' which we do in obedience to the Lord's command and, as such, it cannot bring salvation from sin's penalty.

Space forbids, sadly, from expounding the overwhelming biblical case for salvation by faith alone, upon repentance. We leave it therefore for the reader to satisfy himself or herself that this is the irrefutable mainline teaching of the New Testament, beginning with such texts as John 1:12; 3:16; 5:24, etc. By the way, I'll never forget the sequel to the 2003 seminar we mentioned by way of our opening remarks. As the answers given above were publicly shared, the debaters fell silent and loud 'Amens' punctuated the air in praise of God who had confirmed His Word.

References: (1) Matt.3:11; 1 Cor.12:13 (2) John 3:5 (3) Justin Martyr, Constitutions of the Holy Apostles, Ante-Nicene Fathers, vol.7, p.456-457 (4) Justin, First Apology, chant 61 (5) Ezek.36:25-26 (6) Rom.6:4; cf. 1 Pet.3:21 (7) Rom.6:6 (8) Rom.6:11-12

Bible quotations from the NASB.

CHAPTER THREE: SHOULD I KEEP THE SABBATH? (PETER HICKLING)

You might be rather shocked at the description of Sabbath observance as a deviation from the Christian faith – don't really pious Christians keep the Sabbath strictly? Children of my father's and grandfather's generation were restricted in what they could do on a Sunday to 'keep the Sabbath day holy' (1). Yet before we deplore a decline in standards we should consider what Scripture actually teaches.

The Old Covenant

At the very beginning Scripture says that on the seventh day God finished his work that he had done, and he rested on the seventh day from all his work that he had done. So God blessed the seventh day and made it holy, because on it God rested from all his work that he had done in creation (2). This is what is called an 'anthropomorphism' describing God as if He were a man – because, of course, God doesn't need a rest. However, people do, and God's instructions to His people included many instructions to keep sabbaths; not only the weekly seventh day, but on a number of feast days. The word 'sabbath' occurs 33 times in the Pentateuch (of the ESV), and it is several times described as a Sabbath of solemn rest, holy to the LORD. Any who broke it by working were to be put to death (3).

Why did God ordain this? Part of the reason, of course, was that the day was holy to the Lord, and it gave the people the opportunity to worship him free of daily cares, but partly it was to give everyone a respite from daily work. God said, "the seventh day is a Sabbath to the LORD your God. On it you shall not do any work, you, or your son, or your daughter, your male servant, or your female servant, or your livestock, or the sojourner who is within your gates (4). Remember that in those days there were many slaves ('bondservants' in the old versions of Scripture) who were regarded as property, and their masters could be literally 'slave-drivers', trying to get as much work out of them as they could. Thus the Lord Jesus, picking out this second reason, said, "The Sabbath was made for man, not man for the Sabbath" (5).

Religious rules always offer the opportunity for hypocrisy, and the Gospels give some examples of this. For instance, on one occasion the hungry disciples picked some ears of corn and rubbed them in their hands so that they could eat the kernels (6). The Pharisees criticised the Lord for permitting them to do 'work' on the Sabbath – yet they themselves had many subterfuges by which they could avoid nominal breaches of the Law. They criticised Him for doing the good deed of healing on the Sabbath, although they themselves would rescue their property (7). The ordinance itself was good, but it was perverted by formalistic practitioners into a burden (8).

The New Covenant

The Lord Jesus Himself instituted the New Covenant (9) which superseded many of the practices of the Old. The institution of the covenant itself gave no details about its implications, but Scripture expands on its benefits particularly in the Letter to the Hebrews, which might be expected, since they were the beneficiaries of the Old Covenant. It is important to recognise that the New Testament did not simply render the Old obsolete and irrelevant, but the whole of Scripture contains the developing self-revelation of God to man. For instance, God over the centuries taught His people the necessity of the shedding of blood in animal sacrifices, and the Pentateuch contains detailed instructions about doing this through all their generations. However, chapter 9 of Hebrews shows how the requirement for repeated sacrifices was subsumed in the greater and final sacrifice of Christ Himself; the New Covenant was a 'better covenant', enacted on 'better promises' (10). We cannot here discuss the differences between the covenants, but we can note that God, who gives these covenant promises, has the right to offer something which has greater benefits.

It is as though you had a job paying £30,000 a year and your boss offered you £50,000 with better conditions! The faith of those who lived under the Old Covenant was expressed in the law of commandments expressed in ordinances (11), but that has been abolished through the sacrifice of Christ. Our particular focus is on the question of the observance of the Sabbath, and there our principal guide must be what the new Christians actually did. In practice Christians no longer observed the sabbath, but came together on the first day of the week (12) (our Sunday), because that was the day on which the Lord Jesus had risen from the dead. There was, of course, considerable controversy about whether Gentile believers should have to submit to Jewish ordinances, centring particularly on the matter of circumcision, but that was resolved by the Jerusalem conference of Acts 15, where James summed up, "my judgement is that we should not trouble those of the Gentiles who turn to God, but should write to them to abstain from the things polluted by idols, and from sexual immorality, and from what has been strangled, and from blood" (13)

There was some controversy, too, about the observance of days; Paul wrote, "one person esteems one day as better than another, while another esteems all days alike. Each one should be fully convinced in his own mind" (14). The only particular title for a day, occurring twice in the New Testament is the adjective 'kuriakos', translated in Revelation 1:10 as the Lord's day. It is apparent that there is no scriptural instruction for Christians to keep the sabbath (Saturday), and therefore it would be wrong to insist that it should be done, but it would be equally wrong to put out of our minds the setting aside of a day for the worship and service of God. We live in a primarily secular society, and if it is apparent that we regard some time as the Lord's time it will be as effective a witness as speech.

References: (1) Ex.20:8 (2) Gen.2:2-3 (3) Ex.35:2 (4) Ex.20:10 (5) Mark 2:27 (6) Luke 6:1 (7) Matt.12:11 (8) Matt.23:4 (9) Lk.22:20 (10) Heb.8:6 (11) Eph.2:15 (12) Acts 20:7 (13) Acts 15:19-20 (14) Rom.14:5

Bible quotations from the ESV.

Addendum:

The following are excerpts from previous writings by James Needham (for the entire chapter see The Lord's Supper, Back to Basics, Hayes Press 2014, p.49):

On the seventh day, the people of God both shared God's rest and remembered their own which came in redemption from His hand. By the grace of God, all were to be 'refreshed' in Him, literally 'taking breath' from the toil which sin had brought to the earth. On the last day of the week, the Sabbath had been about looking back on a finished work with restful satisfaction. On the first day of the week – the day on which the last enemy was vanquished – the breaking of the bread looks forward through sorrowful remembrance to the glorious hope of all that His work has accomplished, which shall be revealed throughout the eternal ages and was secured by His resurrection on the first day of the week. In [the Lord's Supper], similarities could be seen with the Jewish Sabbath: it was a weekly assembly; a remembrance of a finished work of redemption which affected all creation; and it was something commanded by and for God. As to the Sabbath, it was a shadow, here was the substance which 'is of Christ'... [But] for all the similarities between the Sabbath and the breaking of the bread, it is in the collective rest of the people of God that the shadow truly finds its substance.

Matthew 11 speaks of rest for the sinner and rest for the servant; Hebrews 4 presents Sabbath-rest for the people of God who Christ Himself leads in their obedience of faith into God's dwelling to worship Him for His Son, so powerfully portrayed in the loaf and cup. The Sabbath initially marked a finished creation; our Sabbath-rest now marks a perfect redemption in which God rests once more, perfectly satisfied with the work of Calvary. Again, He calls men to share His rest, no more a shadow of good things to come, but entering into the very presence of God in the sanctuary, a prelude only to the rest which is eternally ours in Christ.

CHAPTER FOUR: HOW SHOULD CHURCHES OPERATE? (DAVID WOODS)

Ecclesiology? What does that mean?! One definition is 'theology as applied to the nature and structure of the Christian church' (1). The word ecclesiology combines the Greek word ekklēsia, which appears 114 times in the Greek New Testament and is translated in our English Bibles as 'church', 'churches', 'assembly' or 'congregation', and 'ology', which simply means the study of some particular subject. It's therefore the study of churches. But not the study of physical church buildings; ekklēsia always identifies a group of people! With such a proliferation of Christian churches and denominations today, it would seem that ecclesiology is a massive study subject! It would be, if the prevailing landscape of 'Christendom' was our starting point. Our intention is to show that we must start with what the Bible says. Careful study of the New Testament descriptions of churches should determine the form and function of churches today.

We cannot explore every facet in this short chapter, but we will look at some key points relating to church structure, organisation and governance. As we do this, we would ask you to compare the Biblical model with what you see in your local church. The Lord's desire for God-glorifying unity In John 17 the Lord Jesus prayed three times to His Father for His disciples: that they may be one (2). God's desire is for disciples to be united in service and testimony. Where do we see that unity in the Christian world today? Despite what some may say, the contradictory variations in churches point to a departure from God's original ideal; it's not God-glorifying.

Sometimes non-Christians will cite the lack of unity as a reason to reject Christianity. The New Testament shows us that God-glorifying unity is expressed in churches of God in the fellowship of God's Son (3). We must quickly clarify a distinction between 'the church which is Christ's body' (4) and 'churches of God'. All true believers from the day of Pentecost onwards have an eternally secure place, by faith, in the Church which is Christ's Body. It's the church that Christ is building, and not even death can remove someone from it (5). When we read about 'churches of God', however, we're seeing numerous localised and visible expressions of the Church the Body of Christ (6). 'Churches of God' refers to believers gathered together, according to the apostles' teaching, in a given place. Such 'assemblies' would worship God and serve him in ways that would testify to the grace of God in their experience.

Among several notable things that distinguish the local churches of God from the Body, people could forfeit their place in a church of God because of serious sin and rejection of the apostles' teaching (7) but true believers would not lose their eternal place in the Church the Body of Christ.

The First Church of God in Jerusalem – the Model

Following the Lord Jesus' return to heaven, the apostles and other disciples (a group of at least 120 people (8)) received the promised Holy Spirit on the Day of Pentecost. He arrived with a great demonstration of power (see Acts 2 – the Holy Spirit enabling some to speak in foreign languages), and it sparked so much interest that the Apostle Peter used the opportunity to preach to the gathered crowds. The outcome was that about 3,000 souls were saved and 'added' to the existing group. Here was the first church of God – an identifiable, localised gathering of disciples. This church of God was devoted to the apostles' teaching and to fellowship, to the breaking of bread and to prayer (9).

Replicating the Model

As the gospel spread, we see the Jerusalem model being replicated across the Roman Empire. You will notice that a 'church of God' (singular) is associated with a specific town or city location and population (10) If the church of God in a city was large in number they could not possibly meet in one place; we read that the church would meet in various different venues across the city, often in homes (11). Still one church of God, but gathering for the same activities in different venues (12). References to 'churches of God' (plural) (13) are associated with the regional boundaries of the day, Roman provinces. This demonstrates a further unity – when all the churches in a given province are referred to collectively it implies a visible unity seen in all the churches of God referenced. It's interesting to note that when Paul writes about his time as a persecutor of Christians prior to his conversion (14) he uses the singular form: "I persecuted the church of God".

We know that Paul was actively pursuing Christians in towns and cities outside Jerusalem. Surely this is another expression of a wonderful coherent unity across all such churches. How is it possible to maintain such a unity?

Elders in Every Church of God

The apostles had the initial responsibility to pass on the Lord's commands to the first believers. Their teaching became known as the apostles' teaching (15) or the faith (16). Paul said that he taught and directed the same things in all the churches (17) that he expected specifically mentioned practices to be seen in all churches (18) and that he felt the daily pressure of concern for all the churches (19) In time, elders were appointed in each church locality to ensure the continuity of the apostles' teaching, and the careful application of that teaching in local churches.

It's noteworthy that multiple elders were appointed in each church (20). This was to ensure that one man would not take a prominent position or act unilaterally. Paul knew that some elders would depart from 'the faith' (21), so a plurality of elders in each church of God was in part a measure to avoid the introduction of heretical teachings and practices in the local church of God setting. Turning to Acts 15, we see a further unity between elders, this time extending across provincial boundaries. A doctrinal question challenged the earliest teachings of the churches, and a delegation of apostles and elders was sent from Syria to meet with the apostles and elders at Jerusalem in Judea. After debating the matter, a conclusion was reached, which the gathered group was convinced was of the Holy Spirit. This decision was written down and sent back with the delegation to the churches in Syria.

We're told that the same letter of instruction was shared with churches in other regions too with this result: the churches were being strengthened in the faith (22). The important doctrinal decisions made by the gathered elders at the Jerusalem 'conference' were binding on all the churches of God so that God-glorifying unity would be maintained! A brief note about clergy and lay people Paul addressed the Church of God in Philippi with these words: to all the saints in Christ Jesus who are in Philippi, including the overseers and deacons ... (23). There is no mention of any other church 'office' in the New Testament (functions such as pastoring were performed by other gifted individuals (24)).

Paul also warned the Church of God in Corinth about favouring one individual teacher above another (25) in order to avoid division. There was no distinction between 'clergy' and 'lay people' in the first churches of God. In fact, each believer in a church of God is encouraged to exercise their God-given gifts (26) and to participate fully and appropriately in church activities, so that all things be done properly and in an orderly manner (27). Incidentally, the people mentioned in Ephesians 4:11 were given by Christ for the building up of the body of Christ, not as specific 'offices' in a local church of God.

In Conclusion

The outline above summarizes the early structure and governance of churches of God seen in the New Testament. We have no divine instruction to deviate from this model. The New Testament reveals early departures from the apostles' teaching and divisions occurring (28).

History records subsequent disintegration and deterioration as man's ideas, rather than God's instructions, were pursued. The Reformation started a process of recovering lost Biblical truth, which eventually led to the re-establishment of the Churches of God in the late 19th century. Today, these churches, in a true worldwide fellowship, under the God-ordained governance of united elders, seek to honour the Lord's prayer that they may be one.

References: (1) Google (2) Jn.17:11,21-22 (3) 1 Cor.1:9 (4) Col.1:18,24 (5) Matt.16:18-19 (6) see 1 Cor.12:27 (7) see 1 Cor.5-6 (8) Acts 1:15 (9) Acts 2:41-42 (10) 1 Cor.1:2; 2 Cor.1:1; 1 Thess.1:1; 2 Thess.1:1; Acts 20:17,28 (11) see Rom.16:5; 1 Cor.16:19; Col.4:15; Phil.2 (12) Acts 2:44; Acts 4:32 (13) 1 Cor.11:16; 1 Thess.2:14; 2 Thess.1:4; see also: 2 Cor.1:1; Gal.1:2; 1 Pet.1:1; 2 Cor.8:1 (14) 1 Cor.15:9; Gal.1:13 (15) Acts 2:42 (16) Jude 3 (17) 1 Cor.4:17; 1 Cor.7:17; 1 Cor.16:1 (18) 1 Cor.11:16; 1 Cor.14:33 (19) 2 Cor. 11:28 (20) Acts 14:23; 20:17; Titus 1:5 (21) see Acts 20:29-30 (22) Acts 16:4-5 (23) Phil.1:1 (24) see Eph.4:11 (25) see 1 Cor.1:10-15 (26) see 1 Cor.14:26ff (27) 1 Cor.14:40 (28) e.g. 2 Tim.2:17-18

Bible quotations from the NASB.

CHAPTER FIVE: HOW CAN I EXPLAIN SUFFERING IN THE WORLD? (BRIAN JOHNSTON)

"How long, O LORD, will I call for help, And You will not hear? I cry out to You, "Violence!" Yet You do not save" (Hab.1:2). Those words could have been written yesterday by someone on the wrong side of pain and suffering, but they were actually written 2,500 years ago by a Bible prophet. It's been said that no other single issue keeps more people from God – or troubles them so much in their relationship with God – than the issue of suffering. We confirmed that to be the case recently when we were taking the Christian message onto the streets of Leigh, in Lancashire, northwest England. Almost 1 in 5 of the people surveyed volunteered that, if they cared to hear any topic addressed in church, it would be this one. That's in part at least why it's our topic for this chapter. It presents us with both emotional and intellectual challenges, as we'll see.

At 9:02, in the morning of April 19, 1995, Gulf War veteran Timothy McVeigh detonated 4,800 lbs of fertilizer and fuel oil. The resulting blast destroyed the Federal Government Building in Oklahoma, killing 168 people. That bombing was then the largest act of domestic terrorism in the U.S., shattering its pre-911 innocence. Rescue services, as well as bystanders, rushed to pull victims out of the twisted wreckage. As they sifted through the rubble, the small, half-buried body of a critically injured infant was found, and so 1-year-old (Miss) Baylee Almon was thrust into the arms of firefighter, Captain Chris Fields, an image captured by the world's media. Baylee didn't make it, her one name out of the 168 remains with me, since she was the same age as my own son.

But it's not only suffering caused by human atrocities that we need to account for. James Jones, the former bishop of Liverpool, in his book, *Why Do People Suffer?*, tells the story of a school that collapsed when the city it was in was hit by an earthquake. At the school, all the teachers and most of the children were killed. One little boy was badly maimed and rushed to hospital – barely alive. For hours, a team of medics fought to save his life, while his mother waited anxiously outside the operating theatre. After seven hours of painstaking surgery the little boy finally died.

Instead of leaving it to the nurse to tell the mother, the surgeon himself went out. As he broke the dreadful news, the mother became hysterical in her grief and attacked the surgeon, pummelling his chest with her fists. But instead of pushing her away, the surgeon held her tightly to himself until the woman's sobbing subsided and she rested, cradled in his arms. And then in the heavy silence the surgeon also began to weep. Tears streamed down his face and grief racked his body, for he'd come to the hospital the moment he had heard that his one and only son had been killed in that same school.

Assuming the story to be true, as I do, you may still say to me that what seems to be hinted at there, is not an adequate perspective. The surgeon was certainly loving and skilful, but not being superhuman, he was unable to save the child. So, how does that speak to the global issue of pain? For an all-loving God – as per the Christian claim – who is also allegedly all-powerful, could surely have prevented that or intervened in some way. So how do you answer the question: 'Why doesn't God put an end to such misery?' That was the question Olivia put to me on the streets of Leigh recently. And later she took up the challenge and brought her sister Gemma to sit down with a group of us to discuss what the Bible has to say on this profound and poignant issue of pain – which, in some way, touches every single one of us. The Bible does have things to say on it. In fact, it's a recurring theme on its pages and one we shall be exploring as we deal with the intellectual, philosophical, theological and emotional aspects of this troublesome question.

THE INTELLECTUAL CHALLENGE

The most poignant account of suffering in all the Bible is surely the story of Job. Job was an innocent man who suffered terribly. More than 40 chapters are devoted to the account of this one man's suffering: a good man to whom bad things happened. Job accused God of falsely judging him (1); of wronging him (2); of persecuting him (3); of not judging the wicked (4); and of ignoring all his good works (5). It's plain to see Job assumed that God was at fault; while his three miserable friends assumed he was at fault for all the anguished suffering he was experiencing. However, another of Job's friends, Elihu, recognized that, on occasions, suffering can have a purpose. In all his criticism of Job, this more level-headed friend affirmed the sovereignty of God by saying that God doesn't owe it to us to give any explanation for whatever he chooses to do (6). According to some worldviews, people who do good will experience good things, and people who do bad will experience bad things. That's not a biblical worldview, as the case of Job shows. In the biblical view, it's not that simplistic: we can't fully understand why specific suffering befalls us in this life. Job never learned the true cause of his suffering, not even afterwards. Job did, however, encounter God – who basically said to him, "Trust Me." Critics see this as a non-answer to the problem. But that wasn't how Job felt! When Job sees God, it's as if he no longer needs an answer. God Himself is the answer.

Suffering is presented here not so much as a problem requiring a solution; but as a mystery directing us to a Presence. Having said that, in the vortex of pain, whether our own or whenever we're caught up in the observed grief of others, it seems that the most natural question to ask is, 'Why?'. Why did that natural disaster happen? Why did my loved one get cancer? You've been there and so have I, having lost my father to cancer. A friend was telling me recently that it was now over a year since he'd been diagnosed with bowel cancer. He mentioned how, when he was in hospital, a colleague had visited him, and that colleague – most unexpectedly – is now no longer with us. Since then, my friend has undergone surgery and is now fairly fit and well again, and with a reasonable expectation that things will be quite fine. "God is good!" he exclaimed. And God is good. But what if the cancer had taken my friend and it was his colleague who had been the one to survive? Would God be any less good? God would still be good, for that's part of His character which doesn't change.

But we've this tendency to think of God as good only when we get relief from our pain. So, is the reality of suffering – and the existence of evil – a valid argument against the existence of a good God? Let me approach this by asking you to imagine we're called out to a crime scene. A body has been found in the woods, and beside it lies an axe which has been shown to be the murder weapon. You make a mental note that the axe has been finely crafted. A tool, expertly designed for cutting down trees, has been diverted for the purpose of committing a foul deed. You think to yourself: suppose someone argues that because it's been put to evil use – because it has caused suffering – no-one could possibly exist who made it. What a nonsensical argument that would be! For it's clear that the axe has a skilfully machined head, and its handle is an example of exquisite carpentry. True, it's been employed for a wrong use, but that in no way negates the fact that someone made it! That fact is established on grounds other than its use. And it's the same with the case for God. The existence and operation of evil in the world doesn't negate the clear evidence from design which points to a supernatural designer of the universe (an argument endorsed in the Bible, see Rom.1:20). But what kind of God is this creator God who so clearly exists, given that he appears to tolerate evil in the world?

THE PHILOSPHICAL AND THEOLOGICAL CHALLENGES

What can we say about the existence of evil? What are the implications for our belief in God? Far from being a denial of God's existence, as some think – it in fact further strengthens the case for God's existence! How is that, you ask? Take militant UK atheist Richard Dawkins. He argues – and he's being logically consistent – that 'no god' means 'no evil' (7). His point is, if there's no God, then there's no basis for us all agreeing – or even recognising – that something is 'evil'. There could only be individual preferences based on feelings or variable legal opinions. So, taking that same argument in reverse, we can ask: how does the existence of evil actually strengthen the case for God? The full argument runs like this: if there's no God, then there can be no objective moral values. But why, then, is there widespread agreement that events like MH17 (the Malaysian airliner shot down over the Ukraine) are evil? This is a clear indication that objective moral values really do exist, and so God must exist after all – for there's no other way to get them, as Dawkins concedes. But what kind of God is He – if He allows suffering (which is more general than evil, and is not always related to man's inhumanity)? And how is suffering compatible with belief in an all-powerful and all-loving God?

Earlier, I mentioned my friend who underwent surgery. He suffered a lot of discomfort and pain as a result of the surgical procedures. But is he glad that he had the surgery? Yes, of course. There was a morally sufficient reason for the pain and suffering caused by the surgeon – namely, the longer-term wellbeing of the patient. Now, if humans – like that surgeon – can have a morally sufficient reason for causing suffering, then who are we to say that God can't have a morally sufficient reason when He allows suffering? To deny the all-loving character of God, we're going to have to first confidently prove that God could never have morally sufficient reasons. And that's obviously impossible. The Bible prophet Habakkuk cried out to God about the injustice and evil he saw all around him. God answered Habakkuk, but it wasn't the response he expected. In fact, it caused him to suffer more confusion. For God declared that He was about to use a fierce, cruel, neighbouring people to be the instrument of His judgment. Habakkuk then struggled with how God could use these more wicked foreigners to deal with – what he now saw as – the smaller problems of injustice among his own people.

He asked God again, "Why are You silent when the wicked swallow up those more righteous than they?" (8). God responded a second time, declaring that He would settle every score, but it might take longer than Habakkuk was hoping. Until then, He asked Habakkuk to trust Him with the famous Bible words: "the righteous will live by his faith" (9). The remarkable thing is that God enabled him to find joy, even in suffering, for God had provided a morally sufficient reason. And so, Habakkuk did find faith in suffering. That in itself is not unusual. Sometimes, suffering actually brings the one who suffers closer to God. Randy Alcorn in his book (10), says: 'Western atheists turn from belief in God because a tsunami in another part of the world [has] caused great suffering, [but at the same time] many broken-hearted survivors of that [very] same tsunami [have] found faith in God. This is one of the great paradoxes of suffering.' And it's one I've seen with my own eyes on the Pacific Rim.

Talking of tsunamis, natural disasters, and also human-caused disasters, perhaps an illustration may help us to glimpse why the world is now as it is. In 1989, the Exxon Valdez oil tanker ran aground in Prince William Sound, off Alaska. Within hours the beautiful, snowy-white coastline of this previously unspoilt wilderness was transformed by a coating of thick black sludge as 232,000 barrels of oil spilled out from the hold of the stricken tanker. But there was worse to come. Three-quarters of the salmon population that normally migrated to the area did not return the following season. Thousands of seabirds and otters died in this ecological disaster. A place that was originally beautiful had been spoilt by a human blunder. Note, by a human blunder. When a newspaper once posed the question: 'What's wrong with the world?' G.K. Chesterton wrote a published reply which simply said: 'I am.' Indeed, we all are. The world wasn't originally the way it is today, but God gave us the human dignity of freewill, and we shoulder responsibility for how we've used that.

THE EMOTIONAL CHALLENGE

The Times' leader column, the day after the horrific massacre at an infant school in Dunblane, Scotland (on 13 March 1996), said: 'Christ was born among innocent slaughter and died on the Cross to pay the cost of our terrible freedom – a freedom by which we can do the greatest good or the greatest evil.' Early in human history, using our God-given free will, we blundered, the Bible says ... and just like the captain of the Exxon Valdez whom we considered in the previous instalment, we transformed this world into its present mess (11). But this issue is as much an emotional one as it is an intellectual, philosophical and indeed theological one.

In his book, 'The View from a Hearse', Joe Bayly tells the story of two men who came to comfort him after the death of his three sons. The first came with answers. He said that God had a plan, that God could work it out for good, and that God would give Joe strength. The second man simply came to sit with Joe. He didn't speak unless spoken to, but he prayed with Joe and sat in silence alongside him. Joe writes that though both men had good intentions, he couldn't wait for the first man to leave and he couldn't bear to see the second man go. The Bible does have things to say about pain and suffering. But ultimately, the God of the Bible is more like the man who gave his presence than the man who gave his answers.

The Bible leaves many of our specific questions about suffering unanswered. But what it does do, is tell us the story of a God who's drawn close in our suffering – and actually suffered for us – and who will one day abolish suffering forever for those who love Him. I'm reminded of a Church of Scotland minister who was being interviewed by a BBC News reporter on 21 December, 1988, after Pan Am Flight 103 had exploded in the sky over the Scottish town of Lockerbie. The fires were still burning when the reporter turned on the minister and asked, "Where is your God now?" To which the unforgettably calm reply was: "God has joined us in suffering – in the person of His Son, He came as a man, Jesus Christ, and joined us in suffering." He did that when, 2,000 years ago, He paid the price of our freewill and spiritual rebellion on a Roman cross outside the city of Jerusalem in the turbulent Middle East. There's pain at the heart of the Christian message of hope – and it's the pain of God. In all suffering, a question mark remains (for we don't presume to have all the answers); but at the very core of the Christian message, there's not only human pain – the cross of Christ is the mark of divine suffering.

John Stott, after examining other world views, turned from them, and wrote: '... in imagination I have turned instead to that lonely, twisted, tortured figure on the cross, nails through hands and feet, back lacerated, limbs wrenched, brow bleeding from thorn-pricks, mouth dry and intolerably thirsty, plunged in God-forsaken darkness. That's the God for me! He laid aside his immunity to pain. He entered our world of flesh and blood, tears and death. He suffered for us. Our sufferings become more manageable in the light of his' (12) And the poet Edward Shillito said, while looking out on the devastation of war: 'To our wounds only God's wounds can speak'. Another man who looked out over ruins brought about by war was German Chancellor Konrad Adenauer, former mayor of Cologne, imprisoned by Hitler for opposing the Nazi regime, and later chancellor of the West German Federal Republic. Adenauer truly deserves the title of 'statesman', as he picked up the broken pieces of his country and helped to rebuild it in a fractured world.

On one occasion, over against the backdrop of a landscape ravaged by war, he looked evangelist Billy Graham in the eye and said, "Mr. Graham, do you believe in the resurrection of Jesus Christ from the dead?" Graham, somewhat surprised by his question answered, "Of course I do." Replied Chancellor Adenauer, "Mr. Graham, outside of the resurrection of Jesus, I do not know of any other hope for this world." Why? Because the resurrection of Christ, for the believer on Him, guarantees that, for all His followers, there'll ultimately be a pain-free future when an all-loving and all-powerful God – who crucially did intervene 2,000 years ago – will finally wipe away all tears from our eyes (13). Until then, the God who's there draws silently close in love, and invites us to put all our trust in Him.

References: (1) Job 9:20 (2) Job 19:6 (3) Job 19:22 (4) Job 24:1-12 (5) Job 31:1ff. (6) Job 33:13 (7) God's Utility Function, published in Scientific American, November, 1995, p.85 (8) Hab.1:13c (9) Hab.2:4c (10) Alcorn, R, If God is Good, Multnomah, p.102. (11) Rom. 5:12; 8:20-22 (12) J.R. Stott, The Cross of Christ (13) Rev. 21:4

Bible quotations are from the NASB.

CHAPTER SIX: WILL EVERYONE BE SAVED IN THE END? (BRIAN FULLARTON)

The doctrine of universalism, propagated by Origen (185-254 AD), makes the claim that every person who has lived in this world, all through its existence, and no matter their way of life and belief system, will ultimately be eternally saved. Additionally, even angelic beings, who sided with Satan in his rebellion against his Creator, will somehow receive forgiveness and thereby avoid eternal punishment, despite the severity of their sinful actions. The principal logic behind these beliefs is that Christ's sacrifice was a sufficient remedy, and that surely God will be more glorified in saving everyone than in letting Satan be victorious in securing the eternal punishment of multitudes.

Such assertions, of course, run counter to what is clearly and unequivocally emphasised in God's own Word. Moreover, the above logic is faulty, because it presumes we may know better than God, who is all-knowing. Since God is holy and absolutely sovereign, His choice as to who should benefit from Christ's sacrifice is both just and right, and beyond question by His creatures (1). Old and New Testament scriptures indicate that, in His wisdom, God has provided salvation on His own terms, and will be glorified in the outcome. He looks for the action of simple human faith, and the acknowledgement of His absolute authority in, and assent to, what He says and asks for. Unequivocal testimony All earth-born people are classified in

God's Word as rebellious sinners estranged from God: they are all under sin (2). The Scriptures speak unquestionably as to how God will enact His judgement upon those who have openly rejected His will and warnings; they are numerous and we cite but two to validate our understanding and conviction of God's verdict and retribution upon unrepentant human beings and also sinning angelic creatures:

(1) in flaming fire taking vengeance on those (i.e. people of this earth) who do not know God, and on those who do not obey the gospel of our Lord Jesus Christ. These shall be punished with everlasting destruction from the presence of the Lord and from the glory of His power (3)

(2) For if God did not spare the angels who sinned, but cast them down to hell and delivered them into chains of darkness, to be reserved for judgment (4).

Universality of the Gospel

There can be no doubt that salvation is available for all who repent of their sin and place simple trust in the person and atoning sacrifice of Christ. The offer of mercy, forgiveness, and reconciliation is open to everyone, without exception or exclusion (5). Christ has paid the ransom price for the redemption of the human soul, but only those who believe in Him are the beneficiaries. Those who don't, forfeit that promise of pardon and put themselves under the righteous condemnation of a holy God (6).

The Will of God

Some have asked, "Does God get what God wants?" noting that 1 Timothy 2:4 indicates God wants all men to be saved. This scripture is quite accurately translated in the NKJV – who desires all men to be saved. The underlying Greek word 'thelo', translated 'desires' here, indicates the mind and will of God being along a certain direction and Him doing something to achieve the best result without enforcement. (An alternative Greek noun, 'thelema', not used here, is often translated 'will'; it has to do with the determinate and unchangeable decree of the Almighty which, no matter what, will be brought to fruition).

God's desires extend not only to the salvation of souls but also the meeting of just requirements. It is therefore instructive to see that God here uses the word for desire rather than talk about a pre-determined conclusion. God will indeed get what God wants, and His justice and mercy will be perfectly satisfied!

References: (1) Rom. 9:15-16,22-24;11:33 (2) Ps.14:1-3; Rom.3:9 (3) 2 Thess.1:8-9 and see Rev.20:10,15 (4) 2 Pet.2:4 (5) Acts 20:21; Jn.3:15-16; Rom.10:11-13 (6) 1 Tim.2:6; Jn.3:18; 1 Jn.5:12

Bible Quotations from the NKJV.

CHAPTER SEVEN: DOES GOD PROMISE TO MAKE ME RICH? (FRED NTIDO)

What does 'the prosperity gospel' mean? The prosperity gospel is sometimes referred to as the 'prosperity theology', 'health and wealth gospel' or 'the gospel of success'. It teaches that it is the right of all Christians to be healthy and wealthy. This right is presented as based on a covenant relationship which God enters into with all believers at the point of salvation. God is considered bound by His covenant obligations to ensure the health and wealth of all His children. As such, God and the Holy Spirit are considered to be at the disposal of believers to bring about prosperity through positive confession and other 'spiritual' activities such as giving of tithes and offerings to churches and ministries. There are Bible passages which the exponents of the prosperity gospel repeat:

> "...the grace of our Lord Jesus Christ, ... that you through His poverty might become rich" (1)

> "I pray that you may prosper in all things and be in health, just as your soul prospers" (2).

> "But He was wounded for our transgressions, ... by His stripes we are healed (3).

The prosperity gospel is not a recent phenomenon, although it has over time increased in the number of adherents. The message of prosperity preachers centres largely on the hearers contributing financially to their ministries or churches in order to unlock the door to unparalleled wealth and blessings. The yardstick for this is usually Malachi 3:10: "Bring all the tithes into the storehouse, ... and try Me now in this," says the LORD of hosts, "If I will not ... pour out for you such blessing ..." Many of the prominent prosperity preachers are stupendously rich due to the hundreds of thousands and sometimes millions of individuals donating to their churches and causes. They frequently present themselves as proof of the authenticity and efficacy of their message. However, what does the Bible actually teach?

The Bible teaching about wealth and health in the Old Testament Adam and Eve enjoyed unequalled health and wealth prior to the entry of sin. The Lord gave Adam dominion over all living things and he was created to live forever (4). However, with the entrance of sin the dynamics of creation changed: man would die, both physically and spiritually, and he was to labour before he would meet his basic needs (5). There was now no automatic right to health and wealth. In the Old Testament, the Lord reminded the Israelites not to forget that He gave them the power to get wealth (6).

Although He gave specific instructions, compliance with which would usher in material and physical blessings for the individuals, yet there were still poor and unhealthy persons amongst the Israelites and continuing support for these was enjoined (7). The Old Testament is replete with references to the all-sufficiency of the Almighty God and warnings on the danger of a life devoted to the pursuit of wealth (8). The wise man Solomon observed this. Does God promise wealth and health in the New Testament? The New Testament gives clear guidance about health and wealth. The Lord declared: "In the world you will have tribulation" (9). Christians have no guarantee of material and physical ease (10). They are called to a life of self-denial, knowing that they are strangers and pilgrims in this world (11). Whilst some believers may be entrusted with material wealth, it is never for self-indulgence, but for the benefit of others who are less privileged (12). There are repeated injunctions to keep ourselves free from the love of money, to learn contentment and to pursue godliness. The transience of our present troubles (whether physical or material) is contrasted with the eternal weight of glory being worked out for us (13).

The Sovereignty of God

God is sovereign, but the prosperity gospel advocates He cannot do as He pleases (14). He is depicted as a benevolent benefactor at the service of believers who can get Him to act by saying the right words in 'faith'. This 'gospel' is a grave error as it enthrones 'the deity of the believer' who is conferred with similar authority as the Almighty. In the early days of Christianity there appeared to have been elements of this error, as some deemed godliness a means to financial gain and others encouraged the pursuit of material prosperity to the detriment of their spiritual lives. It is to such that the injunction about the love of money being a root of all evil refers (15).

Dependence on God

Scripture admonishes us to work with all our might and to put our trust in God who gives us all things richly to enjoy. We are exhorted to be content with food and clothing and, where blessed with wealth, to employ in it in the furtherance of God's kingdom. We are to store up our treasures in heaven and to know we cannot serve both God and money. Importantly, the Lord Jesus instructs us to guard against every form of greed. Greed is the cornerstone of the prosperity gospel (16).

References: (1) 2 Cor.8:9 (2) 3 Jn.1:2 (3) Is.53:5 (4) Gen.1:28-30 (5) Gen.3:17-19 (6) Deut.8:18; Prov.10:22; Ecc.6:2 (7) Deut.28:1-68; 15:7 (8) Ps.24:1-2; 50:10-12; Prov.28:22; 27:24 (9) Jn.16:33 (10) Matt.8:20; 16:24 (11) 1 Pet.2:11; Heb.13:16 (12) 2 Cor.9:8; 1 Tim.6:17-19; Mk.14:7; Heb.13:6 (13) Heb.13:5; 2 Cor.4:17 (14) Dan.4:32; Is.45:11 (15) 1 Tim.6:10; 2 Pet.2:1-19 (16) Lk.12:15; Matt.6:19,24; Ecc.9:10; Col.3:23; 1 Tim.6:8,17

Bible quotations from the NKJV.

CHAPTER EIGHT: DOES GOD CHOOSE WHO WILL BE SAVED? (DAVID VILES)

At the time of writing, the world was waiting anxiously in the run-up to the US presidential election for the announcement of the final result. It would be momentous, not only for that country, but for the whole globe – the people would make their choice. The winner faces uncertainty about the outcome of his presidency and about the view that history will take of the success or failure of, arguably, the most powerful politician on the planet.

Chosen in Christ

As Christians, by contrast, we may feel like those whom the apostle Paul surveyed in the Church in Corinth: "not many of you were wise ...; not many were influential; not many were of noble birth (1). Yet however we may be ranked by the society or the culture around us, each one of us has been personally picked out – elected – not by the votes of our peers but by the Almighty God Himself. The Bible assures us that each and every child of God has had God the Father voting him or her in – "to an inheritance incorruptible and undefiled ... reserved in heaven for you" (2).

So, for us, there is no uncertainty about a successful outcome, or about our personal mandate – our election is from God and therefore a source of inexpressible encouragement and joy! It is a truth at the very bedrock of God's purposes for each Christian that this act of election was an eternal one, beyond the judgement of history, because it took place before the foundation of the world (3). This is the time, although the word is scarcely relevant in the context, when the counsels of the Godhead were meditated, deliberated and resolved into action. It is the setting for the eternal Lamb of God, foreknown ... before the foundation of the world (4), choosing freely to take on the accomplishment of the whole redemptive master plan of God (5). At this very same time, fellow believer, your name and my name were indissolubly associated with that plan and linked irrevocably with the One who chose to achieve it so gloriously, because at that very time God chose us in Him (3).

When we contemplate the amazing grace of God's election of people such as us in parallel with the mutual choice of His incomparable Son to deal with our sin, are we not moved like Paul to cry, "Blessed be the God and Father of our Lord Jesus Christ" (6)?

Elect According to the Foreknowledge of God

We approach the truth of predestination in Romans 8:30 treading the stepping stones of Scripture, recognising that at each one we are walking on holy ground. The previous verse refers to the foreknowledge of God, a truth which the title of this section (from 1 Pet.1:2) links with our personal election in Christ. Over the Christian centuries, much ink and not a little invective have been expended in endeavouring to balance the twin truths of divine election and God's foreknowledge. To the human mind, election – and predestination – may appear deterministic, allowing little room for human choice, particularly in the matter of salvation. It is the power of choice that makes a person truly human, and the Scriptures make abundantly clear that every individual has that power – for example the Lord Jesus said that anyone can choose whether or not to do God's will (7).

Yet the same Lord also said – emphatically – of His disciples, "All that the Father gives Me will come to Me ... No one can come to Me unless the Father ... draws him, (8) and Luke speaks of as many as had been appointed to eternal life believing (9). These statements make clear that it is not we who choose Christ but He who first chooses us. Some have sought to reconcile these problems into an intellectually satisfying framework by limiting the foreknowledge of God in the matter of salvation to His electing only those whom He knew in advance would respond positively to the Gospel message.

This leaves room for individuals to exercise their own free will to choose according to the foreknowledge of God. The problem with this interpretation is that limiting the power of God in any respect flies in the face of all that He has revealed about Himself to our human minds. His ways are not our ways, and he is not limited by our modes of thought (10). It also fails to do justice to the fact that faith itself, although we clearly exercise it freely at salvation, is nevertheless also the gift of God; Paul emphasises that salvation is a matter of grace (from God) and not of works (by individual choice) (11).

So the faith and repentance of an individual are not the cause of God's choice of that person, but the result. The operation of our will within God's elective purpose is not an easy concept to our limited human minds – we can only accept it by faith. Paul, by the Spirit, helps us with the example of Jacob and Esau (by human standards a simple case of sibling rivalry) by projecting its significance through God's perspective: two baby boys who had no opportunity to choose or exercise faith having the rights of primogeniture reversed so that the purpose of God according to election might stand, not of works but of Him who calls (12).

We are forced to acknowledge the sovereignty of God and the righteousness of all His judgements (13). And to rejoice that, just as the whole course and purpose of the illustrious life of the Lamb of God was foreknown by His Father before the foundation of the world (4), so our less exemplary lives are too.

References: (1) 1 Cor.1:26 NIV (2) 1 Pet.1:4 (3) Eph.1:4 (4) 1 Pet.1:20 RV (5) Is.6:8 (6) Eph.1:3 (7) Jn.7:17 (8) Jn.6:37,44 (9) Acts 13:48 (10) Is.55:8-9 (11) Eph.2:8-9 (12) Rom.9:11-13 (13) Gen.18:25; Dan.4:35 (14) Rom.8:29 (15) Eph.1:4 & 5 RV margin (16) Jer.31:3 (17) Eph.1:9-10 (18) Eph.1:11-12 NIV (19) Eph.1:5-6 (20) Gal.4:5 NIV (21) 2 Pet.1:10 NIV (22) Eph.2:10 NIV (23) Rom.8:29; 2 Cor.3:18; Phil.3:20-21 (24) 1 Cor.2:7-10 (25) 2 Cor.4:10

CHAPTER NINE: MUST WOMEN REALLY STAY SILENT IN CHURCH? (BRIAN JOHNSTON)

The Bible states (1) that women are not permitted to speak when the church gathers together as a church. It is not given to women to lead the church in any audible, authoritative way. This agrees with what we find in 1 Timothy 2:11-12: "a woman must quietly receive instruction ... I do not allow a woman to teach." Yet, quite evidently, many believers throughout the denominations today consider this not to be the case. Let's examine some reasons why some have come to this conclusion:

Claim 1: "This text (1 Cor.14:34-35) is not authentic." However, the text appears in all known manuscripts. It would be irresponsible to try to minimize the force of these verses by doubting that they are original when no manuscript that has come down to us supports the case for their omission.

Claim 2: "The text is not as clear-cut as it appears to be." There have been attempts to play down the force of the statement, even though they are not allowed to speak takes the form of an absolute rule. Some, while agreeing that 1 Corinthians 14:34-35 is both authentic and absolute in character, limit its application to the evaluation of prophecies only. They do this by seeing this as part of a continuing instruction from the preceding verses.

Paul's point here, they tell us, is that the women may not participate in the oral weighing up of such prophecies as he has been dealing with in the immediate context.

But does it not seem inconsistent for those who claim that Paul permits women to audibly prophesy in a church gathering to also say that he forbids them the seemingly lesser task of weighing up the prophecies? The clearer point is that these women were in learning mode (2) and not undertaking any critical or editorial function with regard to freshly-delivered prophecies. For Paul is at pains to ensure that the restriction which he is making does not mean that the women cannot learn. This implies that it was a learning activity in which they were engaged, not the activity of publicly weighing up prophecies.

Paul's summing up actually begins at verse 26 when he proceeds to give practical guidelines for the ordering of both the gifts of tongues and prophesying when the early New Testament churches assembled together. Various in-church speaking roles are then listed in terms of exclusively masculine pronouns until Paul begins to address the womenfolk in verse 34, and then it is in order to explicitly confirm that they are indeed not permitted to speak.

Claim 3: But then, what of 1 Corinthians 11:5? In what sense is the woman there praying or prophesying? The only possible reconciliation with the praying and prophesying women of 11:5 is to understand these women as being part of the overall church company which was engaged in praying and prophesying, but which they specifically were not permitted to lead audibly (3). After all, we today would not hesitate to similarly describe women present at the Breaking of the Bread as collectively worshipping (although silent), being equally part of the holy priesthood.

Claim 4: "This text only applies at that time to Corinth." This argues that the reasons behind Paul's demand for silence are local, probably cultural. The suggestion that some of these women were noisy (or uneducated) cannot be taken seriously, for we must surely ask why, in that case, does Paul ban all women from talking – and were there no noisy men? Since Paul's rule operates 'in all the churches' (vv.33b-34), it would be necessary to assume that all first-century Christian women were noisy which is obviously nonsensical. Some think Paul was advocating a practice unique to Corinth, which means we can legitimately ignore it. Nothing could be further from the truth, Corinth was being asked to come into line with what all the other New Testament churches were already doing. "Has [the word of God] come to you only?" (4).

Paul asks if they are not troubled by the fact that all the other churches have put the same instruction into a quite different ecclesiastical practice. A further argument against this being a statement that speaks to that local culture only is the observation that they are not allowed to speak "as the law says". By this, Paul is probably referring to the creation order in Genesis 2:20b-24, for it is to there that Paul explicitly turns on two other occasions when he discusses female roles in a way which agrees with what we find here (5). The verse in Genesis does not mention silence, but it does indicate that man was made first and woman was made for man, and a pattern has been laid down regarding the roles which the two play.

References: (1) 1 Cor.14:34 (2) 1 Cor.14:35 (3) It is a fact that the Spirit gave prophecy to women to speak, even publicly (Acts 21:9; Luke 2:36-38), but not when the church was called together. The 1 Corinthians 14 portion which begins at v.26 gives an in-church context that is emphasized for sisters in vv.33-35. (4) 1 Cor.14:36b (5) 1 Cor.11:8-9; 1 Tim.2:13

Bible quotations from the NASB.

CHAPTER TEN: IS GOD ONE PERSON OR THREE? (DAVID VILES)

Although defined as 'the central dogma of Christian theology' (1) the term Trinity is nowhere explicitly stated in Scripture. Rather, it is a sublime concept, progressively revealed by God in His Word, which is nevertheless capable of deduction and acceptance by the finite minds of humankind. A classic description is 'one God subsisting in three persons and one substance'. The words 'persons' and 'substance' are highly specific in this context – we will return to them later. Whatever the Trinity means, it must therefore be fundamental to understanding who God is and what God does. The figures one and three are crucial to such understanding.

Christianity will emphatically concur with the Jew and the Moslem that 'the Lord our God is one Lord' (2), but will add that He subsists in three Persons. This fundamental qualification accounts for the continuing opposition of Judaism to Christianity, ever since the Son of God declared, "I and the Father are one" (3). It also places Christianity at complete odds with Moslem monotheism (4). This may already seem remote and complex, but the implications are also fundamental in a much more human way. For John to declare that 'God is love' (5) has little real meaning unless God had somebody to love before He created mankind in His own image – love involves at least two persons.

Jesus insisted that the Father loves the Son with absolute candour and unity of purpose (6). This sublime love, subsisting and streaming eternally between the Persons of the Trinity, is presented to us as the fount of all human love (7).

Explaining the Trinity – Principles

Basic as this doctrine is, it has never ceased to be controversial. For some people, the intellectual difficulty of encompassing a God who is both one and three, is enough for the Trinity to be relegated to the theological back burner or even rejected. There are therefore some basic principles by which the disciple will wish to be guided:

1. We are used to complexity, both in our everyday lives and in the creation around us. Can we expect the Creator – immortal, living in light unapproachable, majestic in holiness – to be any more accessible to our finite minds?

2. The Trinity, like all of Scripture, is the product of divine revelation, and God knows how much revelation we can endure of His ineffable glory. There are secret things which belong only to Him, and surely the fullness of the relationships within the Trinity is one of these. Nevertheless, the things revealed belong to us (8) – assuring us that the Spirit will use meditation on these high and holy revelations to enrich our spiritual lives.

3. There are limitations imposed by our human condition in considering the nature and character of God. One is language, by which God has chosen to reveal Himself, but which is

nevertheless inadequate to the task of communicating His reality. We therefore need to be very careful about the words that we use, recognising their limitations.

Another limitation is our environment, particularly our domination by time. We are driven to use analogies in seeking to explain and defend the Trinity. There is nothing wrong with this approach, provided we are sensitive to the limitations implicit in comparing a thing or a state with the eternal and limitless. For example, in describing the unity and diversity of the Trinity we may choose the analogy of a man who is at once a husband, father and son, uniting three different functions in one person. This is helpful as far as it goes, but it fails to do full justice to the relationships within the Trinity which demand equality and universality as well as diversity (9).

So, confronted by these ineffable facts about God, the humble disciple can only wonder and adore, being content to accept the Trinity as a doctrine which accommodates all the relevant Scriptural revelation. The process thereafter of pursuing analogies which go some way towards explaining it in human terms is legitimate, but to proceed the other way – fitting the doctrine into an allegorical system – is likely to skew and oversimplify any attempt to understand the revealed nature of God.

A little history ... One important example of an unbalanced approach to the Trinity is afforded by the Arian controversy of the fourth century. Arius (c.250-336) taught that Christ, though creator and redeemer, was not of one substance with the Father, being born in time. The root of his error lay precisely in over-emphasising selective Scriptures at the expense of the whole revelation, considering the eternal truths of Christ's divine nature through the perspective of space and time, and in failing to acknowledge the limitations of language in expressing this divine nature. John repeatedly describes the Son as being the only begotten of the Father (10). Arius interpreted this, in conjunction with certain Scriptures implying order in the Trinity (11) in a space/time context so as to indicate that Christ was willed into existence by God.

A similar stumbling block was provided by the Greek word 'hupostasis' in the context of Hebrews 1:3 – the image of his substance (RV) in relation to the nature of Christ. Here is a material word – meaning basis or foundation – used by the Spirit-guided writer in a highly technical, theological sense (12). Arians argued that the Son was not of the same substance, but of a like substance, with the Father, again suggesting that the Son is inferior. So serious were the implications of this teaching, that a Council was held at Nicea in 325 AD, resulting in the famous credal formulation describing the Son as 'begotten not made, being of one substance with the Father'.

A later Council described the Spirit as 'the Lord ... who proceeds from the Father and the Son and with the Father and the Son together is worshipped and glorified.' These classic formulations have stood the test of time, because they take account of the full Scriptural revelation about the Trinity – particularly those which emphasise the eternal existence of the Son in equality with the Father (13) and the divine nature of the Lord the Spirit (14).

These remote debates continue to resonate today. Arian interpretations of monotheism are still propounded by various unitarian groups and by sects such as the Jehovah's Witnesses. And the Nicean debates still leave some loose ends, such as the use of the word 'Person' to describe the Trinity. This word requires cautious use in this context – in the normal sense 'persons' signifies individuals with different knowledge, feelings and will. But in the theological sense, these qualities are all identical (15).

What is God – One in Three

There are many instances, some already referred to (13,14) which make clear the divine nature of the Son and the Spirit, both sharing the attributes of the Father. One particularly noteworthy example is the Great Commission (15) where the risen Lord enjoins the disciples to baptise in one name – God – but in all three Persons. It will have been noted that nearly all the references above are to the New Testament, but it is clear that the Trinity is also at work before the incarnation.

Even in the uncompromising monotheism of Deuteronomy 6:4, the word 'echad' describes 'one' God not in isolation but one in unity, for example as in a bunch of grapes or one people. Turning to the New Testament, it is unsurprising that the work of the Trinity is particularly evident during the 'days of his flesh' – in Christ's incarnation (16), baptism (17) and resurrection (18) and in the act of atonement (19). However, focusing on the essential unity of will and work implicit in the Trinity is only part of the story and can, again, skew our understanding of this sublime truth. Before even Arius, the Sabellians taught that Father, Son and Spirit were only temporary manifestations of the one God, assumed for the purpose of redemption. This error has the apparent virtue of 'simplicity' and is therefore still alive today, but it fails to do justice to the Scriptural revelation of diversity in the Trinity, to which we now turn.

One of the most beautiful and comforting of Scriptures is surely the apostolic blessing (20) This indicates that we are right to discern a diversity of function in the Trinity – in this case, all directed towards us! Other Scriptures point us towards distinctive focuses of the work of each Person (21) and in specific areas – such as creation (22) – particular functions are very evident. Ascribing set roles to each Person (modalism), by which God as Father provides and creates, while in His role as Son He redeems and lives in believers in the mode of the Spirit, is far too restrictive. For example, there are aspects by which all three Persons abide within the heart of the believer (23).

So where do we conclude? While recognising that the Trinity is not to be pigeonholed by our puny minds, we may safely summarise that God reveals Himself to us as God above (24) God beside (25) and God within (26) and that these are particular (but not exclusive) focuses of the respective Persons of the Trinity.

References: (1) The Oxford Dictionary of the Christian Church (2) Deut.6:4 RV (3) Jn.10:30 (4) "Do not speak of a Trinity ... God is only one God, He is far above having a Son." Qu'ran 4:171 (5) 1 Jn.4:8 (6) Jn.3:35; 5:20, cf. Col.1:13 (7) 1 Jn.4:7-21 (8) Deut.29:29 (9) Jn.1:1; 1 Cor.2:10-11 (10) Jn.1:14,18 RV (11) Such as Jn.14:28 and 1 Cor.8:5-6. That there is order in the Trinity is clear ("The Father is greater than I") but, taken with other Scriptures, it is also clear that this does not imply inferiority. (12) The difficulties of rendering this word in a way which is meaningful is demonstrated by the variety of English translations. (13) e.g. Jn.10:30 ("I and the Father are one"): Jn.1:1; Col.2:9 (All the fullness of the Deity) (14) e.g. Ps.139:7; 1 Cor.2:10-12; Jn.14:16 RV ("another Comforter", literally "another of the same kind"); Acts 5:1-4 (15) Matt.28:18-20 (16) Lk.1:35 (17) Lk.3:21-22 (18) Jn.10:17-18; Rom.6:4; 8:11 (19) Heb.9:14 (20) May the grace of the Lord Jesus Christ, and the love of God, and the fellowship of the Holy Spirit be with you all (2 Cor.13:14) (21) e.g. Jude vv.20-21 (22) Gen.1:1-2; Jn.1:3 (23) 1 Jn.4:13-15; Jn.14:23; 2 Cor.1:21-22 (24) Gen.1:1-3 (25) Matt.1:23; 28:20 (26) Jn.14:15-18; Acts 1:8

Bible quotations from the NIV, unless otherwise stated.

CHAPTER ELEVEN: WHAT WILL HAPPEN WHEN I DIE? (BRIAN FULLARTON)

1. An End to Certain Things

(a) Dissociation from our earthly 'tent' (2 Pet.1:14). The apostle Peter was in no doubt that his days of earthly sojourn and service were drawing to a conclusion when he wrote his second letter to fellow-believers in the northern and western parts of Asia Minor. The Lord Jesus had indicated to him many years before certain changes in his physical faculties that would take place through the ageing process, as well as events that would lead to his martyrdom (Jn.21:18,19). Nevertheless, while he was still 'in the body' he would continue his ministry of encouragement before finally laying aside his earthly body, which we all must do eventually unless the Lord Jesus returns beforehand.

(b) Dissolution of our 'earthly house' (2 Cor.5:1) A similar thought of the temporary nature of our earthly existence is expressed here by the apostle Paul, but this time we are taken a step further to be shown that though our present bodily habitation will cease, yet God has prepared an eternal body for our dwelling beyond this present scene, when the burden of the present mortal frame, awaiting something that is far superior, shall be swallowed up of life that will never end (v.4). Paul uses a different word from Peter to describe the separation of body from soul and spirit at death - it is a 'letting go' of that in which we have lived in this world, for the eventual 'taking on' of our eternal body.

(c) Disintegration of our natural body (1 Cor.15:42,44) In speaking of the death and burial of the present body and the later uprising of a new and different body for the believer, Paul has referred to the process of death and life in the agricultural realm, where the sowing ('dying') of a seed that is merely a 'body' of bare grain results some time afterwards in the appearing of a very different entity - wheat or whatever, dependent on the type of seed sown (vv.37,38). In this way we are to understand that although our present body goes back to dust, from which it came in the first place, it has been designed for earthly living alone and has also been contaminated by sin; however, in the resurrection the new body raised by the power of God will far excel in quality the present natural body - it will be spiritual, suited to a different level of living in the life-hereafter, and perfectly attuned to the will of God.

2. Transitions That Take Place

(a) Falling asleep in Christ/through Jesus (1 Cor.15:18,20,51 and 1 Thess.4:13,14). The two expressions reveal the sleep state of the believer's body at death, awaiting the awakening call of the Saviour when He comes again (Jn.14:2,3). Paul has argued his case for the certainty of the resurrection of the believer's body, and its reuniting with the spirit and soul at Christ's coming, based upon the truth of Christ's own rising from the dead. Without the one you cannot have the other; they are interdependent. If Christ hadn't risen, believers who died would be eternally lost. But His resurrection guarantees theirs. Two different prepositions are used, the first 'in' (Gk. en) Christ, relating to their placing as believers as members of His body; the second 'through' (Gk. dia) Jesus, referring to their privilege as beneficiaries of His grace.

(b) At home with the Lord (2 Cor.5:8). This phrase equates with Philippians 1:23 'with (Gk. sun - indicating closeness) Christ', which is said to be 'very far better'. The departed believer enjoys a consciousness of the Lord's presence, in the place where He is: it's His home, and therefore the believer's, too, resting from labours here, and awaiting the Lord's return for His own.

(c) Dead in Christ (1 Thess.4:16) (cp. Rev.14:13 - 'die in the Lord', a reference to future martyrs for Christ during the Tribulation period: see also v.12). This is another description of believers who have left this life; in one of the most stirring passages (vv.13-17 of 1 Thess.4) concerning the resurrection of the saints. Since those in the Church of God in Thessalonica were perplexed about what would happen to those who had died, Paul launches into a step by step description of the actual event of the Lord's return, with those who have died in Christ being in no way disadvantaged; in point of fact they shall rise first to join living saints, then together with them be ushered into the presence of the Lord 'in the air'.

3. The Body of the Believer at Death

(a) Its dishonour (1 Cor.15:43). At the burial of a body, any dignity associated with it in life soon disappears through the process of corruption, it is without honour.

(b) Its debility (1 Cor.15:43) is so very evident too, completely void of strength ('sown in weakness'), an empty shell and nothing more.

(c) Its humiliation (Phil.3:21). The aspect of humiliation is necessarily linked with the effect that sin has had on the human body in life, rendering it ultimately subservient to the onslaught of death.

4. What Will Happen when the Lord Jesus Returns to the Air?

(a) We shall see Him (1 Jn.3:2) according to what John the apostle tells us. The resurrected, glorified body of the believer will have been reunited with the spirit and the soul, fitted perfectly for eternal living.

(b) We shall be like Him (1 Jn.3:2). At last taking on His lovely characteristics and traits the believer will be a most suitable companion for His Lord and Master.

(c) We shall be with Him (1 Thess.4:17) for evermore. This is no mere accompaniment; it is the reality of His presence and our constant proximity to Him in eternity, as conveyed by the Greek preposition 'sun'. First of all, believers shall rise together as one at His coming (again the same preposition in 'with them'), then as one vast entity join the Lord to be led into the 'pleasures for evermore' (Ps.16:11).

CHAPTER TWELVE: DOES GOD FORGIVE DELIBERATE SIN? (JOHN DRAIN)

Questions are frequently raised in connection with Hebrews 10:26, as, for example, "How does God deal with deliberate sin today in the life of a disciple?" or, "Does 1 John 1:5-10 apply to cleanse deliberate sin when that person seeks repentance and confesses?" In approaching these questions, I think we should first examine what we understand "deliberate sin" to mean. Many sins may be committed with the knowledge that what is being done is wrong. The voice of conscience may be heard during or after the committal of sin, but it may also be heard before sin is committed. This means that a person may know that what he is going to do is sinful. If against that knowledge the person persists in his course of action there is an element of deliberateness in his wrongdoing.

But that in itself does not mean that there can be no repentance and forgiveness. When giving instructions to His people Israel in connection with sin and how it was to be dealt with the Lord made it very clear that there were varying degrees of gravity in relation to sin. From these instructions there emerges a very solemn truth concerning what is described as doing anything "with a high hand" or acting "presumptuously". For such sin there was no forgiveness. Such a sinner must die (see Num.15:30; Deut.17:12,13).

I consider that the sinning referred to in Hebrews 10 would come into the category of the presumptuous sin of Numbers 15 and Deuteronomy 17. In Hebrews 10:26 the word "deliberately" carries the thought of what is done designedly with deliberation, knowingly and intentionally. It is the wilful, intentional setting of the human will against the revealed, known and already accepted will of God, and this done, I believe, in very solemn exceptional circumstances. If we examine Hebrews 10:26 in the context of the epistle to the Hebrews we may think of a Jew to whom by the enlightening grace of the Holy Spirit there has come the knowledge and assurance that God has spoken in His Son. He has accepted that Jesus is the Son of God, the Christ, the Mediator and Surety of the New Covenant, the Sacrifice that ratifies it, securing the remission of sins for those who believe and guaranteeing the privileges of the divine service which belongs to the conditional side of that Covenant. These privileges include entrance into the heavenly Holies to worship God through Jesus who is the great Priest over the house of God.

If we think of such a man we think of one to whom has come the realization that all that was foretold and foreshadowed under the Law has found antitypical fulfilment in Christ. Then think of such a person, knowingly and with deliberate intention, repudiating all this and by word and action saying that the divine revelation which he had accepted was a myth, that Jesus was a fraud, that His blood had no more value than that of the malefactors who were on each side of Him at Golgotha. Think of him in so doing offering overbearing insult to the Spirit of grace. Think of him going back to the animal sacrifices and the priestly ritual of a temple which God had forsaken. Adding up all this I think we can see something of what is meant by "if we sin deliberately after that we have received the knowledge of the truth".

How can God deal with such a person? We know that as one who has at some time believed on Christ, accepting Him as his Saviour, the man's sins as a sinner have been borne by Christ and atoned for. They are eternally remitted and will never be seen again. "Their sins and their iniquities will I remember no more", and these sins include past and future at the point in time of conversion. But in Hebrews 10:26 such is the gravity of the wrong that has been committed that God can only abandon such a person to the complete forfeiture of all the conditional privileges of the New Covenant. There is no alternative method by which or basis upon which God can restore the person. He is dead while he lives (see 1 Tim.5:6). Present forfeiture will find future manifestation at the Judgement-seat of Christ when such a person will have the solemn realization that the activities of his life on earth have been burned up. Perhaps we are so carnal that we do not recognize what will be the intense solemnity of seeing at the Judgement-seat that there was nothing for God, nothing for Christ in our lives on earth. Can anything be more grave than this for a child of God? Certainly the physical death of the offender under the Law was not anything so serious as this.

In connection with the matter of repentance I think it is very important to keep in mind the teaching of 2 Timothy 2:25, "If peradventure God may give them repentance". It must not be presumed that men may sin and then by their own decision find repentance. God by His sovereign knowledge knows when and when not to give repentance unto restoration. The prerogative remains with Him. This brings us to another important point. We with our limited knowledge must be careful about reaching a judgement as to when such a sin as that of Hebrews 10:26 has been or has not been committed. As I have indicated above we may commit sins which seem to have in them the element of intention and deliberation but as God sees them they do not have the character of the sin referred to in Hebrews 10:26. Spiritual wisdom, knowledge and discernment will be exercised in seeking to establish whether or not God has given repentance and forgiveness.

1 John 1 refers to children of God who are walking in the light of divine revelation and in fellowship with the Father and with the Son and with one another. They are aware that sin is still in them by reason of the old nature and is ever ready to express itself. But they have the assurance too that the blood of Jesus, God's Son, has an abiding cleansing power. And "He is the propitiation for our sins".

When there is awakened the consciousness of committed sin, and, in consequence, fellowship is affected we have the encouraging privilege of confessing to God who is "faithful and righteous to forgive us our sins, and to cleanse us from all unrighteousness". He knows our frailties, our propensities, our provocations and our trials. In His presence is One who is an Advocate on our behalf and who renders to God full satisfaction for our sins. "My little children, these things write I unto you, that ye may not sin. And if any man sin, we have an Advocate with the Father, Jesus Christ the righteous: and He is the propitiation for our sins ..." To the person contemplated in Hebrews 10:26 no such promise or encouragement is extended. Indeed, that person has repudiated the Sacrifice of Christ.

CHAPTER THIRTEEN: IS IT OK FOR A CHRISTIAN TO VOTE? (LAURIE BURROWS)

The New Testament says nothing directly about political activity for the disciple, but much about divine service. The Great Commission (Matt.28:18-20) is uncompromising; the Lord Jesus said: "All authority hath been given unto Me in heaven and on earth. Go ye therefore, and make disciples of all the nations, baptizing them into the name of the Father and of the Son and of the Holy Spirit: teaching them to observe all things whatsoever I commanded you".

There is a great work to be done by all who would follow in the footsteps of those eleven early disciples who heard the Lord announce this great new service under His own supreme authority. The work of making disciples, baptizing them and teaching the Lord's will for them is very demanding in terms of time and effort. In studying the New Testament, especially the epistles, we find a great deal about discipleship, and in particular how the believer should serve God in the context of the churches of God in the Fellowship of His Son, Jesus Christ our Lord (1 Cor.1:2,9).

Alongside this it is also taught that in the normal course of events the adult disciple should take regular employment, so that he may not be a burden to others but be able to support any family or dependents he may have and contribute towards the expenses of the churches of God and any poor in them, not forgetting to do good to all men (Gal.6:10). In so doing he will maintain a good testimony to those around him (Acts 18:1-4; 2 Thess.3:8-12). It is clear that the kind of employment envisaged here is in order that we may "eat bread", that is, gain a livelihood. It goes hand in hand with spiritual pursuits, is subsidiary to them and has no political objective.

In the New Testament the Christian believer is regarded as a pilgrim passing through this world. Abraham was perhaps the greatest exponent of the pilgrim life, living in tents and looking for the eternal city (Heb.11:8-10). In contrast his nephew Lot longed after material ease and an earthly city. He got what he wanted, became involved in politics and found to his disappointment that he could not influence for good his wicked neighbours (2 Pet.2:6-8). Eventually he lost all his possessions and became a cave-dweller. But Abraham decided to avoid worldly involvement. He turned to God in times of difficulty, and through his supplications Lot's life was preserved when the Cities of the Plain were destroyed by divine judgement (see Genesis chapters 13, 14, 18, 19); truly a clear lesson for today!

Paul tells us to "set our minds on the things that are above, not on the things that are upon the earth" (Col.3:2). He directs our minds heavenward because Christ is there and our citizenship is there (Phil.3:20). "We have not here an abiding city, but we seek after the city which is to come" (Heb.13:13,14). The word "city" (Gr. polis) is an interesting one and its meaning may be of some help in our present study. In the New Testament it denotes a walled town with its own local government structure. From polis is derived a group of English words, including police, metropolis, politics. The derivation of the word politics is not difficult to trace. Leading men of a city would meet from time to time to make suitable arrangements for the conduct of the affairs of the city. They engaged in politics. The wider meaning understood today would naturally follow. In Philippians 3:20 the related word "citizenship" (Gr.politeuma) is used with reference to the life of the city dweller. Paul is here speaking of the heavenly destiny and heavenward attitude of mind of the true believer and exposing the error of those who are preoccupied with material things. In Paul's own words, "their god is their stomach" (NIV); he calls them enemies of the cross of Christ.

The Lesson of History

A fashionable political philosophy maintains that, if the environment is improved, people will be happy and less disposed to crime. This theory ignores the plain facts of the present as well as of the past. In western lands greater affluence has been accompanied by increased crime. Violence of all kinds is the despair of every order enforcing authority, and moral problems have never been so widespread as they are today. Every possible variety of political programme has been tried, but all have failed miserably. Sin always intervenes to spoil the most hopeful of schemes. "Hope springs eternal in the human breast: man never is, but always to be, blessed" wrote the eighteenth century poet Pope, with remarkable insight.

Politicians often labour heroically and thanklessly in pursuit of peace and prosperity. Credit is due to them for their dedication, but failure is in the long run inevitable. The difficulties are too great for human solutions, for man's root problem is the condition of his heart, which is fouled with sin. There is no possibility of bringing peace and contentment to our society until greed and covetousness have been eliminated. These wrongs are innate in man and before wider problems can be approached with any possibility of success there must be the individual cleansing of human hearts. Only the personal experience of the new birth can accomplish this (Jn.3:1-16). That is why Christ went to Calvary, and that is why the gospel is preached. The Son of God did not stoop to manhood and die on the cross as the Sin-bearer for a mere political objective. It was to deal once for all with the all-important, all-embracing problem of sin. And so we return to the point we began with: the Great Commission. The only way to bring lasting good to our fellow men is through the gospel. It is no mere palliative; it goes right to the root of the problem.

The Argument from Prophecy

Even the casual reader of the book of Revelation cannot but be impressed by the dramatic course of events depicted in its prophecies. Much of the imagery may be difficult to understand, but clearly running through the later chapters of the book can be seen the parallel themes of man's mounting opposition to God and the increasing severity of divine judgements on man. Furthermore, in the book of Daniel there are prophetic passages which depict successive world empires dominating men throughout the ages and attempting to challenge divine authority (11:36) until the Son of Man is given the dominion and establishes His everlasting kingdom (7:13,14). World empires are similarly portrayed in Revelation as culminating in an organization, sometimes referred to by present day writers as the ten-kingdom confederacy, led by a king with Satanic power who will oppose God (Rev.17:8-18).

This man will hold sway for a time over the whole world, but he and his centre of administration, Babylon (chapter 18), will be quickly engulfed in a conflagration of divine judgement. Scripture so depicts the great political and religious systems of earth becoming crystallized into one anti-God movement with its centre in rebuilt Babylon. When this world empire reaches the zenith of its power it will be suddenly crushed, completely wiped out, and replaced by a righteous kingdom, enduring for ever, with the Lord Jesus Christ as its King.

Can the Christian support, or vote into power, governments which, according to Scripture, must be at least precursors of the doomed Satanic confederation referred to in the previous paragraph?

Concluding Remark

Involvement of the believer in politics is thought by some to be justified by such scriptures as, "let us work that which is good toward all men" (Gal.6:10). But the verse is to be read in the context of service in churches of God. The conditions which govern the exhortation are plainly stated. Firstly, "as we have opportunity", that is, not as a top priority and not on an organized basis. Secondly, "especially toward them that are of the household of the faith", surely not a mandate to engage in secular political activity! Examples showing the personal nature of the good works envisaged in this scripture are to be found in the word of God. The work of Dorcas (Acts 9:36-43) is eminently worthy of imitation. There is a place for good works in the life of every disciple. Giving a helping hand to those he comes in contact with as occasion presents itself has been found to be a successful method of establishing mutual confidence and rendering an approach to spiritual things possible. In this way the main objective of bringing the gospel to acquaintances can be pursued.

The New Testament sets out clearly what the relationship of the Christian to political systems ought to be. He must be "in subjection to the higher powers" for they "are ordained of God". "Render unto all their dues", writes Paul, "tribute to whom tribute is due; custom to whom custom; fear to whom fear; honour. to whom honour" (Rom.13:1-7). Finally, we have the high privilege of praying for "kings and all that are in high place" (1 Tim.2:1-7). Thus we have access to the court of heaven, where ultimate power over earthly kingdoms resides. God in His sovereignty is bringing to fruition His eternal purposes. In this perspective the greatest of men are of small power, but the believer in prayer has power with God. Our attendance at the prayer meeting will have a greater influence for good in world affairs than attendance at the polling booth.

CHAPTER FOURTEEN: IS IT OK FOR CHRISTIANS TO DIVORCE? (GEORGE PRASHER)

"Heirs together of the grace of life. "This lovely description of harmonious marriage has been true to the experience of countless Christian people. Their marriages, undertaken in the fear of the Lord and guided by Christian principle, have illustrated the wisdom of God in ordaining the life-long commitment of man and wife to one another. The wife's subjection to her husband is complemented by his selfless love for her (Col.3:18,19). Their whole relationship reflects the glorious ideal of the subjection of the Church to Christ, and His matchless love for the Church (Eph.5:22-33).

To all who enjoy the blessings of such experience in marriage the teaching of the Lord and the apostles seems so right, so fundamental. The life-long permanence of marriage gives the relationship a basic security on which all else is built. Nor can there be any question about the consistency of Mosaic provision for divorce, the Lord Jesus took the Pharisees back to the original divine institution of marriage: "Have ye not read, that He which made them from the beginning made them male and female, and said, For this cause shall a man leave his father and mother, and shall cleave to his wife; and the twain shall become one flesh? So that they are no more twain, but one flesh. What therefore God hath joined together, let not man put asunder" (Matt.19:4-6). Such apostolic exhortations as Eph.5:31-33 and 1 Cor.7:10-16,38-40 support these verses.

Sadly, even marriages between disciples of Christ sometimes break down. How sensitive all married partners should be to anything which might spoil the harmony of their relationship! "Take us the foxes, the little foxes, that spoil the vineyards", said the bride in Song of Songs 2:15. Apparently trivial beginnings can lead to serious discord. Neglect of prayer and Scripture reading together may soon undermine spiritual values and blunt our sense of responsibility to the Lord in this area of our Christian life, until gradually the underlying strains lead to open alienation. Or a spouse may yield to moral unfaithfulness, with all its sad and evil effects: trust betrayed, pledges broken, a conscience defiled before God, a loving relationship grievously impaired. What more fruitful cause of marital strain and unhappiness? In 1 Corinthians 7 Paul discusses the strains imposed within marriage when one partner is reached with the gospel and the other remains an unbeliever. Understandably, an entirely new outlook and way of life in the experience of the converted partner may deeply affect the relationship.

So through human weakness and sin, or through changing circumstances, Christian marriage may be put severely to the test. Strains can become so intense that disciples of the Lord Jesus come under pressure to end their marriage by divorce, now so easily available under the civil laws of many countries. Or a Christian disciple may be deserted by an unfaithful spouse who takes divorce proceedings and remarries. In such distressing situations what counsel is there from the Lord? Would He wish His disciple to divorce a partner when strains had made the marriage deeply stressful? Would He permit His follower to remarry if deserted and divorced by an unfaithful partner?

Pharisees were testing the Lord when they asked Him, "Is it lawful for a man to put away his wife for every cause"? (Matt.19:3). The question reflected a division of opinion among Jewish rabbis of that day. One view was that divorce was permissible only when a woman had been guilty of adultery; the other was that she might be divorced for relatively trivial reasons, "for every cause". The Lord Jesus firmly referred to the original ordinance of marriage (verses 4,5) and emphasized its permanence (verse 6). Then His questioners pressed the point that Moses had commanded to give a bill of divorcement, and to put a woman away (see Deut.24:14). The Lord replied, "Moses for your hardness of heart suffered you to put away your wives: but from the beginning it hath not been so" (verse 8). Then followed His notable declaration: "I say unto you, Whosoever shall put away his wife, except for fornication, and shall marry another, committeth adultery: and he that marrieth her when she is put away committeth adultery" (verse 9).

From this discussion with the Pharisees it clearly emerges that the Lord Jesus condemned divorce "for every cause". Indeed, He stated with divine authority that divorce and remarriage should be viewed in the light of what obtained "in the beginning", that is, when God first ordained marriage. Against that divine standard all who remarried after divorce committed adultery, except when the putting away was "for fornication". We shall give further thought to this exception later in the article, but at this point let us note another occasion when the Lord Jesus spoke in similar terms (Matt.5:31,32). He referred to the Mosaic provision for a "writing of divorcement", but re-stated the original standard, and precluded divorce "saving for the cause of fornication".

On yet a third occasion He is recorded in Luke 16:18 as saying: "Every one that putteth away his wife, and marrieth another, committeth adultery: and he that marrieth one that is put away from a husband committeth adultery". So we have this "threefold cord" (Eccl.4:12) in the gospels, statements by the Lord on three separate occasions, each confirming His condemnation of divorce. How seriously we should regard this weighty fact! To us as His disciples His word should be final no divorce or remarriage during the lifetime of one's spouse, "except for fornication". The disciple should not therefore entertain the idea of divorce on such grounds as incompatibility, cruelty, desertion or the like. In some circumstances separation may become inevitable, but in that event the principle of 1 Corinthians 7:11 would apply: "... if she depart, let her remain unmarried, or else be reconciled to her husband".

It has already been noted that both in Matthew 5:32 and Matthew 19:9 the Lord Jesus introduced an exception to His otherwise sweeping denunciation of divorce. Does this exception mean that a Christian may divorce a spouse on the ground of adultery? May a disciple of Christ remarry with a good conscience if divorce has been obtained on that ground? Many evangelical believers have understood the Lord's words in this sense. It has been commonly taught that divorce should be a last resort, that Christian forgiveness should be urged where there has been unfaithfulness within wedlock. But failing repentance and reconciliation the injured spouse may, if desired, take divorce proceedings and remarry.

However sincerely this view may have been held, we are bound seriously to question that the Lord intended to give permission for His disciples to divorce a spouse who had been guilty of adultery, far less to endorse remarriage after divorce. For if that had been His intention one would have expected His statements in Mark 10:12 and Luke 16:18 also to include the exceptive clause. It would seem rather that Mark and Luke were guided by the Spirit to record the Lord's teaching about divorce unconditionally with Gentile disciples primarily in view.

Matthew's gospel is written particularly from a Jewish standpoint, and so Matthew 5:32 and 19:9 include the Lord's reference to Jewish betrothal law. This provided for the putting away of a betrothed woman if she was found to have been unfaithful during the betrothal period, as illustrated in Matthew 1:18-20. For this reason the Lord said "except for fornication", rather than "except for adultery". It should be carefully noted that the Lord is not recorded as using the term "fornication" (Greek: porneia) in a general sense for all illicit sexual intercourse. Rather He distinguished between the two, as in Matthew 15:19 and Mark 7:21,22. In Matthew 5:32 and 19:9 He was using both words in the same context and must therefore deliberately have chosen to distinguish between them. These points are clear from the Authorised and Revised versions of our English Bible, but have been unfortunately obscured in several more recent versions. For example, why should the RSV translate the same Greek word (porneia) as "fornication" in

Matthew 15:19, but as "unchastity" in Matt. 19:9? Or the NIV have "sexual immorality" in Matthew 15:19 and "marital unfaithfulness" in Matthew 19:9?

The foregoing explanation of the exceptive clauses does seem to clarify the principle underlying the Lord's statements about divorce in the gospels. It is not just a matter of the relative seriousness of illicit sexual intercourse before or after marriage. Fornication during betrothal was an act which rendered the marriage void before it came into being. But where marriage had been validly contracted the Lord consistently upheld that there should be no putting away.

We should also notice the disciple's reaction to the Lord's statement see Matthew 19:10. Why were they so astonished? If they had understood Him to say only what one rabbinical school already taught, this would have been no surprise to them. But they were taken aback at the thought of no divorce except for fornication during betrothal not even for adultery, let alone for lesser causes!

Another very weight consideration is the absence of any confirmation from the apostles' teaching that they understood from the Lord that adultery broke wedlock and freed either party to remarry. In view of the major importance of this matter, would we not have expected clear confirmation in the epistles? On the contrary we find such statements as Romans 7:2,3 and 1 Corinthians 7:39 with no mention of any exception on the ground of unfaithfulness within wedlock. Indeed, even when separation becomes inevitable through an unbelieving spouse's deserting a believer, the believer is still enjoined to remain unmarried (1 Cor.7:11).

Nor can verse 15 of 1 Corinthians 7 be construed as giving permission to divorce and remarry. For verse 16 asks a question which refers to each of the situations from verse 12 to 15, a question which would be inappropriate if divorce and remarriage were envisaged in verse 15. "Not under bondage" or "not bound" simply means that the deserted spouse is no longer obliged to press for continued cohabitation.

To conclude that the Lord Jesus forbids the divorce of His disciples under any circumstances, or their remarriage while a spouse is still living, may of course entail stern tests of loyalty to His word. But does not discipleship often involve stern tests in many areas of our Christian experience? "If any man would come after Me, let him deny himself, and take up his cross, and follow Me" (Mk.8:34). Many have suffered persecution, imprisonment or even death for His sake. Others have refused opportunities of marriage rather than compromise the principle of 1 Corinthians 7:39 "only in the Lord".

Loyalty to Christ's word about divorce may bring a difficult test of celibacy for disciples deserted by an unfaithful spouse. Or there may be the heavy burden of caring alone for a young family. The incentives to divorce and remarriage are at times strongly compelling. Yet if for His sake such problems are accepted as a "proof of faith", He will cause all grace to abound as His word is obeyed. Moreover the day will declare the eternal value of placing divine principle before human expedients or natural desires.

CHAPTER FIFTEEN: IS IT OK FOR A CHRISTIAN TO SERVE IN THE MILITARY? (JOHN ARCHIBALD)

This chapter deals with two questions. First, should a disciple of the Lord Jesus Christ join any branch of the Armed Forces? Second, is the answer to the first question altered in a time of war or national emergency when compulsory call up or conscription is in force?

The example and teaching of the Lord Jesus for His disciples must be our starting point and it is very clear from Scripture that the whole tenor of the Lord's life and ministry is sharply at variance with the idea of His disciples wounding or killing their fellow men and women. For example, He said to His disciples, "Resist not him that is evil: but whosoever smiteth thee on thy right cheek, turn to him the other also", and again, "Love your enemies, and pray for them that persecute you" (Matt.5:39,44). Peter also bears witness to this when he says, "Christ also suffered for you, leaving you an example, that ye should follow His steps ... who, when He was reviled, reviled not again; when He suffered, threatened not" (1 Pet.2:21,23). Peter was the man who sought to defend the Lord by force in the garden of Gethsemane, and in so doing he cut off the ear of the high priest's servant. The Lord restored the man's ear and reproved Peter with the words, "Put up again thy sword into its place: for all they that take the sword shall perish with the sword" (Matt.26:51,52). It was one of several important lessons that Peter was to learn in that night of his Master's rejection.

The teaching of the Lord as given through His apostles in the epistles further supports the same conclusion. We find in Hebrews 12:14 the clear instruction, "Follow after peace with all men." Paul the apostle makes it clear that the disciple must have nothing to do with carnal warfare when he says, "the weapons of our warfare are not of the flesh" (2 Cor.10:4), and "our wrestling is not against flesh and blood" (Eph.6:12).

If, as we have seen, the disciple of the Lord has to be a follower of peace who "turns the other cheek" under attack, this pattern of behaviour can only be described as unworldly. In fact unworldliness is a characteristic that the Lord prizes in His followers. "They are not of the world, even as l am not of the world" (Jn.17:16) is how He describes them and desires them to be. The heavenly orientation of the disciple is strongly taught by Paul in his letter to the Philippians: "our citizenship is in heaven; from whence also we wait for a Saviour, the Lord Jesus Christ" (3:20). The Lord Jesus has been rejected by the world. He is a heavenly Saviour and a heavenly King and His followers must also be separate from the world (see Heb.13:12-14).

It is in this context that the Lord said to Pilate, "My kingdom is not of this world: if My kingdom were of this world, then would My servants fight, that I should not be delivered to the Jews: but now is My kingdom not from hence" (Jn.18:36). This statement is a very clear description of the dispensation in which we live. The Lord's use of the word "now" indicates the inauguration of a new period in His dealings with men which contrasts with other periods of men's history when the servants of God have acceptably engaged in earthly warfare. It sets out the difference between the behaviour proper to His followers of today and, for example, the faithful warriors of Israel in the past. Israel was His kingdom (Matt.21:43), and Israel was an earthly people and constituted an earthly kingdom (Ex.19:5,6). It is against this background that we are to understand the Lord's provision for their national warfare, as, for example, in Numbers 1:2,3.

The third line of Scriptural evidence is taken from 1 Corinthians 7:23, where Paul says, "Ye were bought with a price; become not bondservants of men." The meaning of the word translated bondservant is slave or "one who is entirely bound to obey orders at all times without question". Now it is essential in a military organization that there should be absolute and unconditional obedience to human authority, regardless of the nature of the command. The word of the Lord through Paul instructs the disciple of Christ not to put himself or herself in such a position.

Our second questions arises from the fact that when any nation is in a state of war, it is common practice for the government to enlist all able-bodied citizens within prescribed age limits for military service. In this case the individual faces the compulsion of the law of the country to join the armed forces. In the letter to the Romans Paul says, "Let every soul be in subjection to the higher powers: for there is no power but of God; and the powers that be are ordained of God", and again, "Render to all their dues: tribute to whom tribute is due; custom to whom custom" (Rom.13:1,7). Does this mean that if it is wrong for the disciple to undertake military service voluntarily, he or she should nevertheless join the armed forces in compliance with the law which commands enlistment? We believe not.

A careful reading of Romans chapter 13 clearly puts the exhortations to subjection in a civil rather than a military context. This instruction does not apply to a situation where the law of the land directly contravenes the law of the Lord for His disciples. We believe that compulsory call-up to the armed forces does present such a conflict and the guide to appropriate action for the disciple is found in Acts chapter 5 where Peter and his brethren were forbidden by the authorities to preach the gospel. In response Peter and the apostles said, "We must obey God rather than men" (Acts 5:29).

It should be said that in some countries provision for conscientious objection has graciously been made at times of national conscription. Under this provision, opportunity is given to those who object to military service on grounds of conscience to make their case to an appointed tribunal which has power to grant exemption.

In summary, we believe that the Scriptures teach that the disciple of the Lord should not join any branch of the armed forces. If it is wrong for the Christian to wound or kill then we cannot justify that he or she should join even one of the noncombatant parts of the military operation because that would involve direct support of the fighting process and place the Christian in bondage to men. When conscription is enforced by law, the disciple should steadfastly refuse to compromise the position of obedience to the will of the Lord in this matter. Our Master is the Prince of Peace, and we shall best serve the interests of our fellow men and women by faithfully following His example and teaching.

Did you love *15 Hot Topics For Today's Christian*? Then you should read *Sparkling Facets: Bible Names and Titles of Jesus* by Hayes Press!

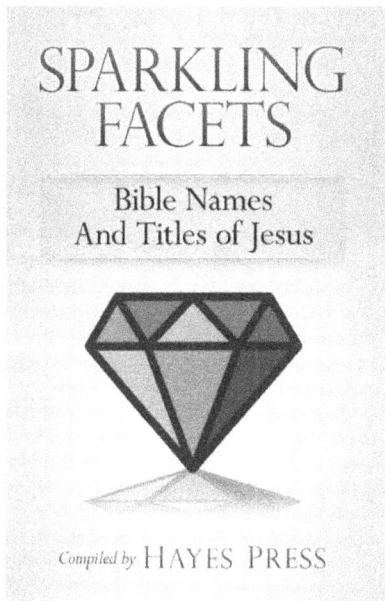

SPARKLING
FACETS

Bible Names
And Titles of Jesus

Compiled by HAYES PRESS

In this devotional and meditational book, twelve different authors write about twenty-six of the names and titles of Jesus, including the Lamb of God, the Son of David, the Great High Priest and the Only Begotten. Some of Jesus' names were given by God, some by men and some He gave Himself, but each name tells us something valuable and precious about His character, His Person or His work.

Also by Hayes Press

Needed Truth 2007
Needed Truth 2008
Needed Truth 2009
Needed Truth 2010
Needed Truth 2011
Needed Truth 2012
Needed Truth 2015
Needed Truth 1888-1988: A Centenary Review of Major Themes

Standalone
The Road Through Calvary: 40 Devotional Readings
Lovers of God's House
Different Discipleship: Jesus' Sermon on the Mount
The House of God: Past, Present and Future
The Kingdom of God
Knowing God: His Names and Nature
Churches of God: Their Biblical Constitution and Functions
Four Books About Jesus
Collected Writings On ... Exploring Biblical Fellowship
Collected Writings On ... Exploring Biblical Hope
Collected Writings On ... The Cross of Christ
Builders for God
Collected Writings On ... Exploring Biblical Faithfulness
Collected Writings On ... Exploring Biblical Joy
Possessing the Land: Spiritual Lessons from Joshua
Collected Writings On ... Exploring Biblical Holiness
Collected Writings On ... Exploring Biblical Faith
Collected Writings On ... Exploring Biblical Love

These Three Remain...Exploring Biblical Faith, Hope and Love
The Teaching and Testimony of the Apostles
Pressure Points - Biblical Advice for 20 of Life's Biggest Challenges
More Than a Saviour: Exploring the Person and Work of Jesus
The Psalms: Volumes 1-4 Boxset
The Faith: Outlines of Scripture Doctrine
Key Doctrines of the Christian Gospel
Is There a Purpose to Life?
Bible Covenants 101
The Hidden Christ - Volume 2: Types and Shadows in Offerings and Sacrifices
The Hidden Christ Volume 1: Types and Shadows in the Old Testament
The Hidden Christ - Volume 3: Types and Shadows in Genesis
Heavenly Meanings - The Parables of Jesus
Fisherman to Follower: The Life and Teaching of Simon Peter
Called to Serve: Lessons from the Levites
Needed Truth 2017 Issue 1
The Breaking of the Bread: Its History, Its Observance, Its Meaning
Spiritual Revivals of the Bible
An Introduction to the Book of Hebrews
The Holy Spirit and the Believer
The Psalms: Volume 1 - Thoughts on Key Themes
The Psalms: Volume 2 - Exploring Key Elements
The Psalms: Volume 3 - Surveying Key Sections
The Psalms: Volume 4 - Savouring Choice Selections
Profiles of the Prophets
The Hidden Christ - Volumes 1-4 Box Set

The Hidden Christ - Volume 4: Types and Shadows in Israel's Tabernacle
Baptism - Its Meaning and Teaching
Conflict and Controversy in the Church of God in Corinth
In the Shadow of Calvary: A Bible Study of John 12-17
Moses: God's Deliverer
Sparkling Facets: Bible Names and Titles of Jesus
A Little Book About Being Christlike
Keys to Church Growth
From Shepherd Boy to Sovereign: The Life of David
Back to Basics: A Guide to Essential Bible Teaching
An Introduction to the Holy Spirit
Israel and the Church in Bible Prophecy
"Growth and Fruit" and Other Writings by John Drain
15 Hot Topics For Today's Christian
Needed Truth Volume 2 1889
Studies on the Return of Christ
Studies on the Resurrection of Christ
Needed Truth Volume 3 1890
The Nations of the Old Testament: Their Relationship with Israel and Bible Prophecy
The Message of the Minor Prophets
Insights from Isaiah
The Bible - Its Inspiration and Authority
Lessons from Ezra and Nehemiah
A Bible Study of God's Names For His People
Moses in One Hour
Abundant Christianity

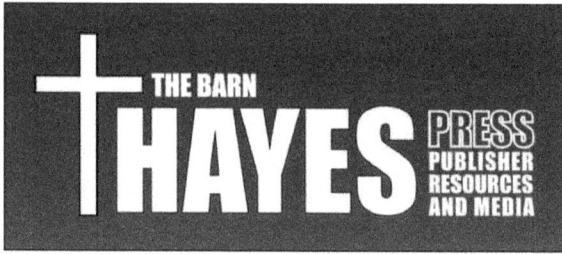

About the Publisher

Hayes Press (www.hayespress.org) is a registered charity in the United Kingdom, whose primary mission is to disseminate the Word of God, mainly through literature. It is one of the largest distributors of gospel tracts and leaflets in the United Kingdom, with over 100 titles and hundreds of thousands despatched annually. In addition to paperbacks and eBooks, Hayes Press also publishes Plus Eagles Wings, a fun and educational Bible magazine for children, and Golden Bells, a popular daily Bible reading calendar in wall or desk formats. Also available are over 100 Bibles in many different versions, shapes and sizes, Bible text posters and much more!

www.ingramcontent.com/pod-product-compliance
Lightning Source LLC
Chambersburg PA
CBHW020511030426

42337CB00011B/339